D1291963

ARE
YOU
THERE

God?

AMIDST THE **DARKNESS**
LOOK TO THE **LIGHT**

CHARISSE JONES

WESTBOW
P R E S S®
A DIVISION OF THOMAS NELSON
& ZONDERVAN

Copyright © 2020 Charisse Jones.

All rights reserved. No part of this book may be used or reproduced by any means, graphic, electronic, or mechanical, including photocopying, recording, taping or by any information storage retrieval system without the written permission of the author except in the case of brief quotations embodied in critical articles and reviews.

This book is a work of non-fiction. Unless otherwise noted, the author and the publisher make no explicit guarantees as to the accuracy of the information contained in this book and in some cases, names of people and places have been altered to protect their privacy.

WestBow Press books may be ordered through booksellers or by contacting:

WestBow Press
A Division of Thomas Nelson & Zondervan
1663 Liberty Drive
Bloomington, IN 47403
www.westbowpress.com
1 (866) 928-1240

Because of the dynamic nature of the Internet, any web addresses or links contained in this book may have changed since publication and may no longer be valid. The views expressed in this work are solely those of the author and do not necessarily reflect the views of the publisher, and the publisher hereby disclaims any responsibility for them.

Any people depicted in stock imagery provided by Getty Images are models, and such images are being used for illustrative purposes only.
Certain stock imagery © Getty Images.

Scripture quotations taken from The Holy Bible, New International Version® NIV® Copyright © 1973 1978 1984 2011 by Biblica, Inc. TM. Used by permission. All rights reserved worldwide.

Scripture taken from the King James Version of the Bible.

"Streams in the Desert" 366 Daily Devotional Readings by L.B. Cowman 1997 Zondervan, Grand Rapids, Michigan pgs. 235-236

ISBN: 978-1-9736-8969-0 (sc)
ISBN: 978-1-9736-8971-3 (hc)
ISBN: 978-1-9736-8970-6 (e)

Library of Congress Control Number: 2020906611

Print information available on the last page.

WestBow Press rev. date: 04/14/2020

I would like to give all honor and glory to God for giving me the ability, strength, and perseverance to write this book. Without the gift of writing and passion for serving God, there would be no book. I look forward with anticipation toward how God will continue to pour into me so that I may pour into the lives of others and build His kingdom.

Contents

Acknowledgments

I would first like to thank my loving family: my husband, Marlon, who has always pushed me to know who God is; and our two sons' Corin and Caden. Your love, support, and encouragement are a testament to how much you love Jesus. You all are mighty men of God and I love you dearly.

I would like to thank my mom, Charlene, for being my biggest cheerleader. As I grew older with the responsibilities of an adult, wife, and mother, you were always there to give guidance, wisdom, and unconditional love. There is no greater love than a mother!

I would like to give thanks to my pastor, Bishop Bronner. You are indeed a man of God leading God's children to come to know Him. During these past fourteen years of attending Word of Faith Family Worship Cathedral, my spiritual life has grown immensely. I have not only come to know Jesus Christ as my Lord and Savior but also seek to live out this Christian walk depending on Him completely. The seeds of biblical knowledge that you have planted God is most definitely watering for my victory and His glory!

Preface

In this journey, we call life; God has given all of us a story that we can share with others. Communicating through writing may or may not be your avenue to share the love of God, but best believe God wants every person to testify to His glory. Our experiences and adventures, failures and successes, test, and trials are all different. But one thing is the same; we all come to know Jesus, eventually. God gives us free-will to accept Him and our Christian walk, but Jesus' existence does not change because of our choices.

I grew up knowing and believing in God but was far from experiencing a personal relationship with Him. And with lack of Spirit to Spirit intimacy, I could not witness how God's Divine hand protected, provided, and directed me. However, when pain and hurt lurk into your soul and mind, there is no better time for God to step in, introduce Himself, and show you who He is and who you are. So, out of hurt, pain, fear, and the desire for change in my life came my ministry.

The birthing of this book expresses how God's love and

light illuminated through my experiences during the years of my foolishness. It provides a practical application illustrating life events, which helped me to see God. I hope by sharing my various life stories, it will help you reflect on your encounters and see where God was and still is in your life.

After recognizing our Heavenly Father and His ever-existing presence, this compelled me to share my story, to inspire, and lead others to Christ! I started out blogging weekly inspirational devotions, but always knew in my gut and heart of hearts, God commissioned me to write a book. Life is hard and unfair sometimes, but God wants to help you in this journey. What we go through is nothing new to God, and He has the best solution to help push you forward. However, gaining God's help means we first need to acknowledge that He exists. An ambulance does not come to your house unless you call 911, you do not get an interview for a job until you complete an application; you do not lose weight until you change your eating habits and exercise. I think you get the picture. Relationship requires reciprocity, which is a mutual exchange between you and God. Each party has their part to play, and your role will take some trust, obedience, hope, and faith in an omnipotent, omnipresent God.

I hope that as you read this book, you will begin to recognize, encounter, and embrace the living God who longs to be your lifelong partner. This life we live, God never intended for us to experience without the companionship of Jesus Christ. God loves you so much that He gave His only Son (John 3:16) for your sins, for your present existence, and your future eternal salvation.

PART I

The Past

1

I Did Not Really Know Him Back Then

We all come to know the Lord at different times in our life. Whether during contentment, happiness, emptiness, pain, depression, health problems, financial issues, loss, or just riding high on the mountaintop, God can infiltrate our existence. He is the Creator; I Am, the Omnipotent One. Not time or circumstance influences His abilities or authority.

For me, the unquestionable acknowledgment and revelation of God's greatness, love, and protection happened in November 2006. In my time of distress, God gave guidance, peace, and love that was indescribable and unattainable by humans. Before this, I knew of God's existence but only from a customary religious standpoint. I went to church occasionally, prayed before I went

1

to bed, and blessed my food before eating. Honestly, my bedtime prayers consisted of praying while in the bed with one eye open fighting back sleep until I could gasp the final 'amen.' Did you notice I said "amen" not "in Jesus Christ's name, amen!" Living a life of ritual habits did not afford me the luxury of becoming exclusive with the God who took the time to give "His one and only Son" for me (John 3:16) and knows me by person (Jeremiah 1:5).

So, what happened on this typical November day to cause me to seek God and know Him for more than just an empty prayer life? Well, you could say my "come to Jesus" moment happened when I made the wrong job move instead of waiting on God. Not knowing that God wanted me to "be still" and wait on His divine plan, I moved anxiously to a job position that doubled my salary but had future ramifications that changed the trajectory of my life. However, this paradigm shift opened the door to an awareness of our loving, faithful, gracious, and merciful God who would pick me up, dust me off, and place me on the right path. Even though money was the motive for my hasty job choice, "God worked all things out for my good" (Romans 8:28) –and a genuine, sincere relationship was first on His agenda. Now you're probably thinking, *Why was this a bad decision? You increased your salary.* "*God wants His children to prosper!*" Yes, He does want us to prosper but not at the expense of excluding Him and His protection. Scripture tells us in Philippians 4:6–7, "Do not be anxious about anything, but in every situation, by prayer and petition, with thanksgiving, present your requests to God. And the peace of God, which transcends all understanding, will guard your hearts and your minds in Christ Jesus." Being a Christian who occasionally attended Sunday service (the only day I read the Bible) did not allow me full access or understanding toward the magnitude of purposeful Christian living and following Jesus Christ. Turmoil day in and day out, heartaches, headaches, embarrassment, and depression resulted from this job choice because I did not consult God.

Even though family and friends could console me, my pain and depression increased each day I went to work. During this time, a coworker who knew my struggles gave me a devotional book called *Deserts in the Storm*. As I began reading each daily devotion, it was as if God was speaking to me (the broken place in my heart) and my situation. I was growing through this ordeal. I began to call on the Holy Spirit, and He invaded my space emotionally, mentally, spiritually, and relationally. It was then I realized that I did not know God for the love, compassion, strength, and power He possessed and wanted to share with me. It was in this special time with God that I gained strength, wisdom, and peace through my circumstances and storm. The hardship at work never changed because the goal was to develop me, the individual, not improve my surroundings. God was invading my space and transforming me to become what I declared to be, a child of God. As each year went by, things got worse and worse with my boss causing me to press harder into God's Word and presence pleading for His help. I made a vow to myself and God that I would read the Bible from beginning to end so I could be armed with His truth and follow the example modeled by Jesus Christ. Gaining His truth helped me to understand that whether a modern-day Christian or the chosen people, the Israelites, we all must seek to know Him.

As I reflect on my lack of knowledge about God, it makes me think about the Israelites in the Old Testament. Over two thousand years ago, God claimed a chosen people, the Israelites. Exodus 3:15 tells us that God is the God of Abraham, Isaac, and Jacob, so even though the Israelites were enslaved people, they were God's chosen nation. However, the Exodus account gives the illusion that neither the Israelites nor Moses really knew God at first. At the burning bush, God commands Moses to free the Israelites. But Moses responds, "Suppose I go to the Israelites and say to them,

The God of your fathers has sent me to you, and they ask me, what is His name?" (Exodus 3:13).

How can a claimed nation not know who the living God is? Was not the God of impossible miracles talked about through the generations? Did the Israelites not believe in the God who gave children to the old and barren, promising a great nation from twelve tribes? My perception was that neither Moses nor the Israelites were intimately acquainted with God; however, God fully knew who His people were and how He planned to save them. As the Israelites cried out because of their oppression and slavery, God heard their plea and remembered His covenant with Abraham, Isaac, and Jacob (Exodus 2:23–24). God performed ten impossible, supernatural miracles that no person could execute. Each day His mighty hand warned the Egyptians and strengthened the Israelites' belief. God not only freed His chosen people from slavery but also kept every promise toward their prosperous future and has not changed His position for the modern-day Christian.

So how did God, whom I did not recognize because of my ignorance, make Himself known to me? By coming into my situation, circumstance and somatic chaos uninvited but ready to heal, comfort, love, free, and accept me for the sinner I am. What I discovered through my impatience and dysfunctional job was that my lack of willingness to submit to the Holy Spirit hindered my awareness of the presence and will of God. Without knowing God, I had human thoughts and actions instead of spiritual, life-giving progress. I reacted to several fleshly thoughts throughout my young adult years; however, my time and season had come to acknowledge God and stop living in mediocrity. It was time for me to recognize my Creator, who is my source, strength, and pilot.

As spirit-beings, we are image-bearers of the one, true God (Genesis 1:28) and purposeful on this earth. But to discover our purpose, we must become acquainted with God, and this can only happen by the pursuit of the One who holds our lives in His hand. To know Him is to seek Him, find Him, and develop the character of the One who lives inside us and with us (Matthew 7:7). God is omnipresent, dwelling in the nooks and crannies of our ordinary lives, and if we do not stop to recognize and submit to His presence, we will continue to live and search for the unimportant.

2

Every Tub Has to Sit on Its Own Bottom

At a young age, I heard the cliché, "Every tub has to sit on its own bottom." I never really understood what it meant, but when I got older, I became acquainted with this relevant saying. Are you the kind of person who can always be so diligent helping others with their goals and dreams, planning their steps, but sometimes lack the tenacity to get things done in your life? Have you ever wanted something so badly for someone else, but they chose a different path? Yup! Is that what you said? Me too! Join the club. Trying to help plan everyone's future in my household hindered me from seeking my own goals and dreams. I could see the potential in my spouse and children for their passions and talents, research what they needed to do, make the phone calls, and help them get started, but somehow I'd drag my feet on what was pulling my heart-strings. So, not only did I stagnate my dreams, but I placed unnecessary stress and frustration on myself because of their choices. Now isn't that funny! But that is a real problem because God has prepared good works for all His children to perform (Ephesians 2:10). And it is our responsibility to figure out our God-given talents through prayer, intimate time with God, and godly wisdom.

It was fall semester 1990 and time to complete my application process for enrollment into the nursing program. I had completed several prerequisite courses for the nursing program and reached the status where I could apply for core nursing classes. My mother and I completed the application together. I also wrote an essay describing my aspirations and goals for wanting to become a nurse. Check, done! No problem writing that essay because working in the medical field was a lifelong dream for me. Becoming a pediatrician was my career goal. A few weeks had passed, and I received a letter in the mail revealing the fate of my future in the nursing program. I remember feelings of excitement, anxiousness, and fear of the unknown response. I ran upstairs to my dorm-room, closed the door, and ripped open the envelope. When I opened the letter, my heart dropped, and I felt an ache in the pit of my stomach. They denied my acceptance into the nursing program for the fall semester. I remember crying like an infant child, hungry and longing for the touch of their mama. As I calmed myself down, I called my mother to tell her the news. When she answered the phone, I began to cry uncontrollably, gasping for air, and articulating the words 'they denied me!' My mother was furious but comforting, feeling the pain of her daughter's dreams crushed. As long as I can remember, my childhood dream was to become a pediatrician because I loved to interact and take care of kids. When my mother's friends would come over to the house with their children, I would always watch the babies and sit for hours holding and feeding them, and even changing a few diapers. I remember having such a connection with children I wanted to take care of them, hence my reason for enrolling in the nursing program to become a doctor. I had a plan, and with the help of my mother, I would complete my 4-year bachelor's degree with credentials in nursing then move onto medical school. However, after receiving the denial letter, all my medical dreams flew out the window, so I thought. But! My mother's fury and tenacity was the pivotal action that changed my denial to acceptance. She contacted the school, spoke to the head of the nursing department, and got my fatal decision revoked. She was my superhero, and I love her dearly for that!

I started the nursing program excited, ready, willing, and able. News flash! This academic journey of life-searching and seeking required that I start at the bottom and work my way up. And, why did I think learning the dynamics of medicine would be any different? Achieving the credentials of a doctor meant I had to learn the fundamentals of a nurse. In the nursing program, my first intern assignment involved working in a nursing home with elderly patients. *But what about the babies I loved to care for and cuddle!* I practiced giving and receiving shots. *But could not stand the sight of blood nor being shot with a needle!* I was in the books studying day in and day out. *But what about the fraternity party my roommates plan to attend!* I had 8 am labs and long class days. *But what about sleeping in late and afternoon classes!* Come on, I mean, this is college, home away from home. Don't I get to set my schedule! Suddenly, I began to reflect on where I was going with this profession and my unhappiness toward my career direction as immaturity became the culprit for my irrational thinking. However, the constant news flash of mom's perseverance with the nursing department to change their decision became an ever-present reminder. But, God knew my character flaws before pursuing the medical field, and that denial letter could have just been a blessing in disguise. However, I saw the denial letter as a disappointment, and my mother felt her child's pain, so God allowed us to press forward learning and gaining a valuable life-lesson. I completed one year in the nursing program and changed my major the following school year. Reluctantly, I told my mother the news after leaving nursing school and starting a new program. What was back then is now 'a tub sitting on its own bottom!'

My mother was disappointed because she knew that at a young age I talked about becoming a pediatrician. Still, she understood that as an adult, the decision was mine to make. Even though she saw my potential and compassion in caring for babies, she wanted me to be happy with my career choices. So she supported my decision and told me to do my best.

My best is what I did, but it took many years to accomplish because I did not have a plan B. The medical field was my only career plan, thus, resulting in changing my major a few times and taking a break from school. During this break, I worked, which meant I was making money and not thinking about school. However, I needed to finish what I started, and climbing the corporate ladder would require a degree. Therefore, after my long sabbatical, I completed my bachelor's degree and walked across the stage as a wife and mother.

Having my children brought back the nurturing feelings I once had when I was young proclaiming to become a doctor. So, immediately after completing my bachelor's degree in Business, I pursued an Education degree and became a schoolteacher. Somehow, I believe this was God's direction for my life from the beginning. However, my disconnection with God led to misdirection in my life. My mother wanted the dreams I expressed the desire to achieve, but 'every tub has to sit on its own bottom.' I had to search my heart of hearts where God lives for the authentic purpose and calling on my life. After eighteen years and counting of teaching, I have learned something else about myself. I-LOVE-WRITING! All those years of being a student and teaching students developed my writing skills. Absorbing scripture nurtured my spiritual maturity and wisdom, which helped me to see how God's Word applied to my life.

Now, as a parent of two beautiful boys, I see with the eyes of an ambitious mother for her children. Does that ring a bell! As my mother was my cheerleader years ago and still to this day. I am gunned-ho for what my children say they want to become and a cheerleader in their corner willing and ready to help my boys plan the navigation of their lives. My older son says he wants to work in film and video, so as his number one fan, I have guided him in that direction. And, as I assist him with his dreams, I can identify with my mother's encouragement and letdown when she supported me all those years ago. He has made significant progress toward his aspirations of working in the filming and video industry. Still, I have thought he should be further along than he is, a mother's intuition! However, I must remind myself that in my years of college, I did the same thing. After getting into the nursing program, I realized that I did not want to work in the medical environment. It was my responsibility to make a life decision just as it is my son's responsibility to be accountable for his life decisions. As with my spouse, he has shared his dreams and aspirations with me. Again, I would offer suggestions, make calls to get the ball rolling, and ask questions toward what he had performed to reach his desired outcome and move his dreams in the right direction. Honestly, I will probably do the same thing with my younger son. He says he wants to be a mechanical engineer, and at his school, they have a robotics club along with a few engineering courses. We have already discussed his intentions and spoke with the teacher in charge of both programs.

Do you see a pattern here? I really cannot help myself. Yet,

I am learning that support does not mean 'do it for them.' And understanding this vital factor can help minimize any frustrations I cause for myself. In my case, support means I do all the planning and research and give you the information - now get it done. But, in the realm of spirituality, I must "train up a child in the way he should go: and when he is old, he will not depart from it" (Proverbs 22:6 KJV); therefore, as my spouse and children spend time with God, He will give them the direction, guidance, and wisdom they need to persevere. If I learn to take my hands off the steering wheel, God will direct.

In the life of Samson from the Old Testament, we see similar life experiences between parents and their children. Nurtured values instilled and supported by the parents became personal decisions impacting the child's future. In the Book of Judges, "there was a man named Manoah from the Danites clan and he and his wife were childless, but the Lord showed compassion on them and gave them a son. God gave specific instructions on how the mother should eat during pregnancy including how the child should be raised. Samson was to be a Nazirite, dedicated to God, and a deliverer for the Israelites against the Philistines" (Judges 13:3–5). Besides the leadership responsibility Samson would gain, God told his parents never cut the child's hair; a command Samson would also need to follow.

As the story climaxes, Samson's parents obeyed the Word of God as they reared their son. Teaching him God's commands and his Nazirite culture, the Lord would bless Samson with a purpose that would save the Israelites from their oppressors. But, just because parents offer wisdom and experience to help their children with life decisions, 'every tub has to sit on its own bottom.' Samson would make his own decisions, which lead to volatile actions, intercultural relationships, pride, and disobedience. His trickery antics caused him to disobey God, lose his hair, and the power of

God, thus becoming a prisoner of the enemy, the Philistines. How did God's anointed fall so far? I would say solely by his decisions. Even though Samson's parents trained him according to God's commands, Samson had to make his own decisions. And rightfully so we all have to make our own decisions. But, if those decisions do not include guidance and direction from God, we can best believe that our consequences will be the manifestation of harrowing experiences.

As I grow in my spiritual maturity, I understand that we all come to Jesus in our own time and way. When we are on the outside looking in, we can see a person's potential, but we do not know or understand what it takes to be in that person's shoes. We do not get to feel the desires, failures, wants, or discouragement that anyone experiences while living out their life of aspirations. Every person's testimony is different, but a diligent, novice relationship with God can develop into a fulfilling, transformational, and long-lasting connection that promotes godly decisions and direction. Thus, we obtain the wisdom of responsibility and accountability through our purposeful choices and actions.

3

Reflect on the Past but Do Not Stay There

Circumstances and situations in life may set us back for a moment. Still we must continue to persevere, making a conscious decision to move forward because only then will we be able to rise pass the test of our situation and tread ever-consistent toward victory. Reflecting on the past but not staying there means considering your past actions and consequences with a more mature perspective surrendering all hurt, pain, rejection, and burden to God, trusting that He will heal your wounds (Jeremiah 30:17). Reflecting means, we learn from our mistakes and failures to make better decisions the next time.

Frequently Scripture reveals Jesus reflecting not on the past but the future and choosing to surrender His Will for His Father's Will.

While Jesus was in the Garden of Gethsemane, He asked God "to take this cup away" (Matthew 26: 39, 42, 44). But instantaneously changed His attitude and posture towards His Heavenly Father's purpose for His life and humanity by saying "not my will but your will be done" (Luke 22:42), and we must do the same. Jesus' words are not focusing on the past because He foresees, and honestly already knew His future suffrage on the Cross. However, Jesus shows a moment of human weakness, as we all do, to illustrate how we should surrender all things to God. Witnessing human weakness in Jesus shows us how to deal with our hurt and pain in a godly manner with Christ-like character. Jesus decrees, "Come to me, all you who are weary and burdened, and I will give you rest. Take my yoke upon you and learn from me, for I am gentle and humble in heart, and you will find rest for your souls. For my yoke is easy and my burden is light" (Matthew 11: 28–30). As Jesus declares, "learn from me" (v.29), this demonstration of submission toward God's Will should help us understand and perceive that Jesus is teaching us a way to deal with our inward battles. By changing His thought process to God's Will, Jesus mitigates His feelings toward the difficult task before Him pressing toward the ultimate glory God would gain.

How Jesus changed His thought process in mid-stream, exemplifies the identical transformation we must fix our thoughts to when living in and dealing with the past. You might ask, "If Jesus is Lord, why did He display human weakness?" And in response, I would say, to show us that as human mortal sinners weakness compels us all, but through His example, we can persevere. We can make it! We can get over the hurt, pain, betrayal, segregation and racism, and lack by posturing ourselves toward the alive, active God (Hebrews 4: 12). You can make it!!! What we see from the example of Jesus is that His demeanor stayed in a "go, do, move" position because He knew that His life served an ultimate purpose for God's glory.

As living beings, we all have a past to deal with and overcome. We all have made mistakes we regret and choices that we wished we could take back. But, without our failures, bad decisions, and successes, we could not learn from those consequences to make wiser decisions and share our testimonies. When we reflect briefly, and I say briefly, because our past need not become our today and future, we can gain a constructive perspective for positive present and future outcomes.

I am no stranger to past hurts, disappointments, or adverse experiences. I have experienced pain in relationships, finances, through ignorance, pride, ego, selfishness, teeter emotions, and the list goes on. However, what I have been noticing about myself is that reflection on my past is allowing me to make different choices or shall I say godly decisions for my future. Mediation fosters spiritual maturity that repents for sinful decisions that cause hurt, disappointment, and pain toward self and others. It bears witness to others so they can learn from the mistakes of their neighbor steering in the opposite direction of repetitive generational curses. Conviction encourages a prayer life that prays for another chance, not a second chance because we blew our second chance years ago, thus becoming more fruitful and obedient in our present and future existence.

In my late teens, around-about my second year of college credit cards used to come in the mail pre-approved and all you had to do was use the card to establish ownership and accessibility. This particular year, I received five pre-approved credit cards in the mail, and being the starving college student that many of us are, I used each of those cards creating debt for myself. I was a non-working college student; therefore, when I received each monthly bill, who did I think was paying my "minimum" payment. You noticed I said minimum balance and not paid in full. Also, back in those days, minimum payments for college students was around five dollars, and five dollars a month did nothing for a balance totaling thousands of dollars.

My use of these five credit cards went on for about a year, and my plan to make that measly minimum payment was to get a student work-study job along with occasional cash advances to pay the monthly bill. Did you catch that? I made more debt to pay debt. Do you see anything wrong with this picture? Can you say starving, ignorant college student.

Fast-forwarding to a complete year of credit card ownership, my mother somehow found out I had five credit cards. She repossessed every credit card in my possession taking away my lucrative cash flow and paid all the balances down to zero. Thank God for loving, caring mother's with ignoramus children. But my stupidity did not end there. My mother kept the cards for years until she felt I was mature and responsible enough to handle the cards. How about this level of accountability did not hit me until my twenties? I was now an adult out of college, still using credit cards, frivolously, and approaching the possibility of bankruptcy. How injudicious could I have been to not learn from the mistakes I made in college? My first mistake was acquiring five credit cards, knowing that I had no real job to support my spending habits. My second mistake was not respecting the blessing and help my mother gave me by paying my debt. And, my third mistake was taking the same impulsive path of spontaneous spending, as I did as a teenager, and not using this wisdom as I approached motherhood, marriage and a life of real personal accountability. Had I reflected on my past spending habits and what financial pain this caused me, maybe just maybe, I could have made different decisions? Little did I know that my lack of judgment as a young adult would impact my future growing family negatively; a young-minded, indulgent action with future consequences. Instead of reflecting and redirecting my future back then, I chose a life of self-gratification, which has now become the guardian of wisdom for me today.

Since then I have become wiser about my financial habits. Nothing like discomfort to encourage astuteness about money handling. God's Word tells us to "Let no debt remain outstanding except the debt of love to another" (Romans 13:8), and "the borrower is the slave to the lender" (Proverbs 22:7). I can tell you from experience that I have been more times than none a slave to Visa and MasterCard, but this circumstance does not have to consume my future or life.

In the Book of Matthew, Jesus tells a parable about the bags of gold. Jesus explains that a man went on a journey and left his wealth to his servants. The man gave his servants bags of gold according to their abilities, skills, or tenacity, which I like to think. The man with five bags doubled his bags to five more. The man with two bags also increased his bags to two more, but the man with one bag did nothing with his bag. He did not spend it or save it. Scripture says he dug a hole in the ground and hid the gold. He just let it collect dust until the owner returned (Matthew 25: 14–18). You're thinking, what does this parable have to do with financial pain or reflecting on the past? A lot! The servant who did nothing with his money received harsh criticism for his money-handling habits. The master called the servant "wicked, lazy, and worthless" (Matthew 25:26, 30). Not only did the master call him names, but he also took the servants one bag of gold, gave it to another servant, and dismissed him from his work duties (Matthew 25: 14– 30).

When I reflect on how this parable impacts my financial habits, I can see that God expects us to handle money wisely and proficiently. God wants us to have a mind of excellence, not wickedness, to work and not be lazy, to know the significance of our gift and talents not deeming them meager or worthless. Therefore, God is a God of multiplication, not subtraction or stagnation. The servants with five bags and two bags doubled their bags- multiplication! Their efforts pleased their master. Therefore, not exercising your skills to become fruitful is a subtraction in the economy of God. My frivolous debt accumulation not only subtracted what I had, but I also became a slave to the lender for my impulsive spending habits. Sometimes it is necessary that we face reality and be real with ourselves not to sugarcoat our mistakes. And in this chapter it is important I speak learned wisdom not just to you but to myself.

Now, just for disclaimer, I do not profess to be a financial advisor or even an expert of the Bible. But, I have gained wisdom from experiences that have caused me to reflect on past decisions to make wiser, godly choices. I seek to gain discernment and understanding from God so that my present life and future are fruitful, my children's life is fruitful, and your life as you read this book is fruitful. I am sure you have heard the cliché, "experience is the best teacher!" Well, experience is a great teacher, but God is the only teacher that gives grace and mercy to overcome past mistakes. And this can only happen with transformed, godly thinking. God is the only one that can help you have an abundant life that is fruitful, joyful, peaceful, and loving.

4

What Did God Tell You to Do Last

Do these words sound familiar to you? "What did I tell you to do?" As parents, we have probably said this very phrase a million times to our children. If you are not a parent, then in your childhood years, you have heard these very words from your parents. However, as a believer in Jesus Christ, can you recall God instructing you to do something? How did you respond? Was it something like "yes…, I do not want to…, later…, or maybe you just forgot?" What was God's last command or Word, which you still have yet to start?

As I sat in God's presence, reading my Bible and writing my thoughts, I remember saying these words, "I will do it!" My morning routine comprised waking up in the tranquility of a peaceful house before the organized chaos of cooking, cleaning, working, and

21

running errands begun. One might say the typical "mom" routine, not to alienate the vital job of a husband and father, but I needed to get up early before household pandemonium occurred. Besides, getting up before the hustle and bustle of the house, I would isolate myself for at least an hour studying God's Word basking in the Holy Spirit, so the rest of my day was productive and guarded with God's wisdom. However, before leaving my sanctuary place this one particular day, I remember feeling in my spirit that I should write a book. Earlier that week, I had been listening to various podcasts about using your gift and that gifts from God were not gifts unless I shared them with others. Immediately I thought about the godly wisdom I gained through life experiences and my Bible study time. These thoughts lead to visions of various book titles and topics that I would write to help and inspire others in this journey we call life.

My morning routine of spending time in God's Word had been going on for years, and I could tell that my understanding of the Bible had changed. It was as if God was opening my eyes and revealing knowledge to me I had not been privy to before. Now, just to backtrack a moment, I believe my understanding and wisdom grew because I asked God to help me discern His Word. One regular Sunday as I was listening to the pastor preach, I asked God to give me the understanding and discernment of His Word like the pastor. Thinking about that now, I did not know the responsibility and accountability that would come with this tall order I requested. I remember saying, "Lord, I'm not asking to be a pastor but to understand your Word (the Bible) like the pastor so I can gain your wisdom." And, that precisely is what God did, each year after that prayer request, God revealed His wisdom and knowledge to me. I know this to be true because not only did God open my eyes to His Word, but He also orchestrated life events that I needed His help to persevere. I felt so honored that God not only answered my prayer but also trusted me with His wisdom to understand how He expects all His children to live and come to know Him. Scripture tells us that, "If any of you lacks wisdom, you should ask God, who gives generously to all without finding fault, and it will be given to you" (James 1:5); thus, God kept His Word and answered my prayer.

Now, back to how God transformed my thinking. As I went about my day, everything I experienced, whether at home, work, or just through the ordinary course of the day, became an experience that I could see God's hand, scriptural relationship, and something to share with others. Thus, the manifestation of a vision for writing inspirational literature developed through spending time with God and nurturing my God-given gift. So, now here's where the phrase, "What did God tell you to do last" comes into play. Even though I had these thoughts and occurrences regularly, I never picked up my computer to write. I replaced the feeling of writing a book with pursuing academic ventures and even creating a blog webpage. I figured that I could obey God with my blog writing, which was more my speed. As days became weeks, months, and even years, I continued to make excuses and occupy my time with goals that did not surmount to anything and hindered my progress toward the inevitable. Are you running from your God-given gift? Are you replacing a command with comfort? Now five years later, I find myself sitting here writing you this book on my fears, failures, triumphs, and successes all in the name of Jesus Christ. Had I listened five years ago, there's no telling where my life or my family's lives would be right now. There is no telling how many other books I would have written, including the many people I could have impacted from back then to now. But there is good news! God is good and faithful! He gave me time, knowing that I would be right here at this point in my life writing this book now. And guess what? I will even share a story in the Bible, showing how history repeats itself.

Are you familiar with the story of Jonah and the fish? Well, in this story, God gives a man named Jonah a specific command, and he presumes not to follow God's request.

"The Word of the Lord came to Jonah son of Amittai: Go to the great city of Nineveh and preach against it, because its wickedness has come up before me. But Jonah ran away from the Lord and headed for Tarshish" (Jonah 1:1– 3). Throughout the story, Jonah experiences some unfavorable events because of his disobedience toward God's command. Not only did Jonah not listen to God, but he also compromised other people. Jonah boarded a ship to flee to another city, and his defiant behavior caused the entire boat and crew to witness the measure of God. What made Jonah think he could run from God in the first place? Had he not heard about God's miraculous signs and wonders in the past? What about you? Has what God told you to do last, affected your family, significant others, or those around you? I can raise my hand and say, "Yes, Sir!" Scripture says that "Jonah boarded the ship and as it sailed God brought a violent storm with great winds that threatened the ship and the sailors" (Jonah 1: 4– 5). Is disobeying God worth the affliction because of your choices, including the other people it may impact? Has your disobedience caused others to experience loss, whether physical, mental, emotional, spiritual, or financial? As the sea raged and the sailors feared for their lives (*emotional and psychological impact*), they began throwing cargo overboard (*economic impact*), hoping to lighten the ship's capacity to handle the waves better.

However, the storm continued to rage because the culprit for this roaring downpour was not the sailors but Jonah. The ship and sailors were just innocent bystanders who got caught up in a lousy scheme of disobedience. Has your noncompliance to God's Will caused others to feel sorry for you and try to help you? Have the efforts of others been unsuccessful? Thus manpower is no power against God's power! The sailors determine that Jonah is the reason for the terrible storm. Jonah tells the men to throw him into the sea, but the men do not want to sacrifice Jonah's life, so they try to row back to land opposing Jonah's wishes.

Now, I do not want to get totally off track of this teachable moment, but I would like to share a life experience to support this biblical text. When I taught first-grade years ago, we performed a butterfly experiment during our butterfly life cycle unit. The kit came with a cylinder netting, about ten caterpillars, and food. As the caterpillars climbed the net, they would nestle in a spot to transform into a chrysalis. Also known as a cocoon. After days of metamorphosis, the culmination of this process is a beautiful butterfly. However, the focal point is not the butterfly life cycle. It is the stages and processes that take place for the butterfly to become an independent creature. When a butterfly is breaking out of its dwelling, you are not to help it in this process. The wings are damp, so trying to assist the creature will either damage its wings or cause the butterfly not to build up strength to fly. Either way, as the students watched the butterfly scuffle for freedom, his struggles prepared his wings and body to undertake the dynamics of flying. Can you figure out what I'm trying to say? Like the butterfly, Jonah needed to go through this full measure of struggle with God because it would encourage him to seek God more sincerely and repent for his disobedient actions.

As the sailors struggled with rowing against the storm (*physical impact*), they all agreed to throw Jonah overboard. After a desperate prayer from the sailors (*spiritual impact*), who did not know the one, true God, they threw Jonah overboard, which caused the raging sea to silence. Witnessing a raging sea become calm caused the sailors to believe in God, offering sacrifices and vowing their loyalty to Him (Jonah 1:13–16). Now, how about that? God received glory and praise through disobedience! What the sailors witnessed caused them to worship the real, true God and not a false god. And, Jonah had his turn to worship God because he ended up in the belly of a fish for three days and nights. He could do nothing but pray to God for repentance, forgiveness, and another chance to obey. Will praying to God in repentance and forgiveness alter your circumstance? Know that God is only a prayer away! In Jonah's time of remorse, God heard his prayer, and the fish released him in the great city of Nineveh. Did you notice that God had the fish release Jonah at the city He commanded? Nineveh was the city that God commanded Jonah to preach His word. It was in Jonah's suffering and sorrowful heart that his only plea and care was to listen and obey God. Jonah's prayer was a prayer of distress, help, mourning, gratefulness, promise, and obedience to our loving Father. Scripture says that after Jonah prayed, "The Lord commanded the fish, and it vomited Jonah onto dry land" (Jonah 2:10). It was easy for God to command the fish because He created the fish. God can command anything on this earth because He is the Creator. So, regardless of your disobedience or mine, God can change our situation with a spoken word.

Can you imagine being in the belly of a fish for three days? Personally, when I think of fish, the first thought that comes to mind is the fish on my plate, which I intend to eat not eaten. However, as I think about all the different whales I have seen in the aquarium, I could not fathom being alive and sitting inside a fish gazing its interior walls. That would scare the living daylights out of me. I can see myself in a full-effect "come to Jesus" moment pleading for freedom. But, I believe in Jonah's case, he was so remorseful towards his disobedience that being in the belly of a fish was his last thought. I think God had Jonah's full attention, and Jonah was ready to obey so God could get the glory.

What is your belly of the fish experience? How did God get your full attention? Or is He still seeking your attention? How did or will you respond? Believe me, if you have not had your belly of the fish encounter, it is on the way if you are a believer in Jesus Christ exercising your 'free-will' with a gift that God intends to use for the building of His Kingdom and glory. Even if you are not a Christian, you too can have a belly of the fish experience, which will bring you to acknowledging and seeing the one, true God for Who He Is! Besides, if you are reading this book, this means you are human and not exempt from the issues of this world.

For me, this encounter hit me like a mac-truck when I lost my job in 2018. I was living a life of contentment in a comfort zone that did not enhance my gift or abilities. Honestly, it was complacency because, personally and spiritually, there was nothing challenging about the work I performed. I grew more frustrated with the redundancy of my job as the years passed. Through all this, I only posted weekly inspirational devotions on my blog, never intentionally sitting down to write my book. But remember, God will ask you, "What did I tell you to do last?" So, do not be surprised if your "fish encounter" directly results from your lack of zeal with God's request.

As I continued to talk with God about my aspirations of doing more for His Kingdom and how my job was a 'good' distraction, low and behold God's gavel hit the sound block, and my employer eliminated my job position. So, are you wondering, "What is a good distraction?" Here's my interpretation of a good distraction. It is when you have something going on in your life that is positive, whether relationship, job, school, etc. but it stagnates your real purpose. A good distraction will provide knowledge and maybe even enhance your skills because we learn from every experience; nonetheless, it is a distraction that eats up valuable time and detains our genuine assignment. And time is something we can never get back. As I continued to have these conversations with God about my purpose and removing distractions so I could be more productive, the job and the security-net I thought I had vanished. If you ever think your job or career is your security, please think again. God is our only source who provides the resource!

Nothing like walking on water with Jesus (Matthew 14:29) or being in a fish's belly because you did not listen to the last instruction or maximize your time wisely. Before losing my job, I complained daily because the reality of my life was the same year after year. My discomfort elevated as I noticed years of no change in my life. But I had not changed the rules of my game. I went to work during the day, as a schoolteacher, and then came home and logged onto my computer as an online instructor. I was living a mundane existence feeling that God could use me for something greater. Life was ordinary, and I accepted mundane-living because it was comfortable, but we are Christians with a gift in hidden treasures (Isaiah 45:3) to use for the building up of God's Kingdom. Therefore, the only way we will find our hidden gift is by spending time with God, preparing, and answering the call.

Are you wondering what this has to do with what God told you to do last? Probably not because the title should speak to your heart and mind bringing you to conviction as it did me. But if you wonder, then that means you need to reread these few pages and pull out your Bible. Get in a quiet place and posture so that God can speak to your heart. Then Act!!!

Seriously, this story depicts how we as Christians hear God's voice, whether through dreams, visions, conversations, heartfelt passions, or His Word, but do not move on what He has instructed us to do. We do things our way saying to God, "Are you sure? Do I have to? That will take too long! I do not have the resources! I do not have the time! I need it now!" But God is saying, "Trust me! Have Faith! Do not worry about the how or just do not worry! I know you're scared, but I got you! I will be with you! You can do it!"

God is our biggest cheerleader because He has already prepared the way for our victory, success, and growth (Ephesians 2:10), not to mention He created you and knows all your capabilities. So, stop waiting! What did God tell you to do last? For me, it is writing this book and any other book; God gives me the wisdom to write. Start that business or nonprofit organization, write that song or novel, become that dancer, artist, chef, doctor, lawyer, student or begin that ministry, whatever it is do it! It will not only bring glory to God but also fulfill your desires. So together, let's move on what God told us to do last and watch His hand move favorably in our lives.

PART II
The Present

5

Do Not Focus on the Blessings of Others, Celebrate

How's your attitude meter? How do you respond to others when God showers them with blessings? Are you genuinely happy for them? Do you congratulate? Or do you wonder why not me? Well, the title of this chapter alone is enough to encourage you to operate within your purpose-driven lane, which reduces stress and anxiousness. When we see others receive blessings from the Lord, we should not focus on it to the point of self-pity, hater-ism, or bitterness, but celebrate with that person because of God's goodness and faithfulness. However, I must admit I have looked at the blessings of others thinking, "Lord, why haven't you blessed me? Why is it taking so long? When will I receive what I prayed for?" But over the years, I have learned that concentrating on the blessings of others is just a distraction from the enemy to get you off God's plan for your life. When we focus on others and their successes or growth in life, it encourages broken focus toward our personal development. If the achievements of our peers do not ignite a peculiar passion for development, you will continue to believe the grass is greener on the other side. God's Word tells us that "He will give us hidden treasures and riches stored in secret places for us" (Isaiah 45:3) but to obtain those blessings, we must focus on God, seek His plan, and stop emphasizing on the benefit or shall I say, "lives of others!" Know that "God's thoughts are not our thoughts nor His ways our ways" (Isaiah 55:8– 9). "He is not a human that He should lie or change His mind... What God speaks He acts upon and fulfills His promise" (Numbers 23:19). So, it may just be that your plans and mine are too minuscule toward what God has and wants us to do. God wants to give you a bigger blessing, which requires you to stop looking at others and redirect your focus to Him. So, eliminate the gossip and minimize the social media surfing on Instagram, Snapchat, Twitter, Pinterest, and Facebook so you can get into the "good book" called the Bible. Anything that causes you to believe someone else has a better life eradicate these thoughts from your mind. "We must continue to think about such things that are true, noble, right, pure, lovely, admirable, excellent and praiseworthy" (Philippians 4:8).

Now I am no stranger to looking at other folks "grass," thinking why is theirs so green and plush, but my grass looks like crabgrass with weeds and flowers I did not plant. I can recall two instances where two of my friends' careers just took off, but mine stagnated for years. In 2002, I decided that I wanted to become a teacher, so I went back to school to get my Master's degree in education. You remember, a few chapters earlier, I wanted to become a pediatrician, but I learned through trial and error that this was not the profession for me. However, after having children and being a part of their educational journey, the love for working with kids came back, so I pursued a career in education. I applied for a job in my local school district and started working as an assistant teacher, also known as a paraprofessional. As I worked as an assistant teacher, I pursued my education degree so I could become a certified teacher. During this time, my good friend and past coworker inquired about the school I was attending to receive my teaching credentials. She talked about changing careers and felt that teaching would best suit her personal and family needs. So, I supplied her with the appropriate information, and the two of us went through our teacher courses together. I was about six months ahead of her, and we became a support team keeping each other accountable to our educational goals. We both graduated from the program and worked in our local school districts; however, it took me a much longer time to become a primary teacher than her. She even set me up with an interview at her school, but to no avail, I continued as an assistant teacher for years. Now to go back just a little, after I graduated from the teaching program, another friend of mine who worked in the corporate sector also wanted to become a teacher and inquired about the school I was attending. Again, I assisted this friend with all the information needed, including some textbooks I had purchased from my previous courses. Upon her graduation, she too became a primary teacher quickly or at least quicker than my process. So, one friend worked on her degree while teaching elementary students in her local school. The other friend worked on her degree and was an assistant teacher, but transitioned into a primary teacher position quickly after graduation. In both cases, I questioned God and focused on their instantaneous blessing of becoming a primary teacher.

Honestly, I harbored this resentment for years and not toward my friends, but with God. I not only saw my friends accomplish their goals and succeed to this day but also saw countless other colleagues move into positions I felt equally qualified to perform. But, who said I wasn't qualified, Not God! Their grass was not greener than mines. I nurtured and mowed my lawn just as they did. I worked very hard to achieve my Master's degree, including assisting each friend. But I learned after years of maturity that I was where God needed me to be, and He loved me beyond my resentment and pride. Not only did my degree help me in diverse areas of the education field, but God also had me to be a conduit for their paths, which impacted their lives and families. I take no credit for their progress or success because each friend worked very hard to get where she desired. I only sowed the seed, but God watered and gave the increase.

You know, God requires us to help others and sometimes what looks like your path can be a channel to bring others through. As I focused on the blessings of others because my route took me around so many curves, I missed how God was blessing me to accomplish greater heights. My path allowed me more freedom, family time, authority, and personal time with God. Now, why should I complain about that?

As I was thinking about the bases of this chapter and understanding the importance of focusing on what God has for you and celebrating other's blessing, the affectionate prayer Jesus professed in the Garden of Gethsemane came to mind. I mentioned this prayer in an earlier chapter; however, God reveals and expands my understanding of His Word in varied ways. Thus, He allows me to take the same scripture and provide a different, eye-opening revelation to it. So, how does this story relate to hater-ism against other's successes, stressors of reaching goals, anxiousness toward your aspirations, and bitterness toward people or God? Well, let's just say, the example Jesus illustrates in this story is one that minimizes personal will for God's Will. In the gospels of Matthew, Mark and Luke, we have a depiction of Jesus praying to His Father.

As Jesus is praying, knowing that He is about to die for the sins of the world, He petitions God by saying, "My Father if it is possible, may this cup be taken from me. Yet not as I will, but as you will" then in a few verses further, verse 42, Jesus proclaims "if it is not possible for this cup to be taken away unless I drink it, may your will be done" (Matthew 26: 39 & 42). Jesus, already knowing what the Father required of Him, did not have to pray this prayer. He knew and prophesied to the disciples that He would die for the sins of the world. Jesus knew that Judas would betray Him, the details of His prosecution by the Jewish leaders, how the disciples would scatter and deny Him, and how God would raise Him from the dead. So, this prayer shows the importance of focusing on God and His purpose for us. Had God granted Jesus His Will to take the cup away from Him, then Jesus would not have died for our sins. It is my understanding that only a small circumference of Jews would have known and seen the glory of God through the miracles that Jesus performed because they were eyewitnesses. There would be no world atonement or salvation; thus, the enemy who reigns today would have the victory. However, Jesus' full-knowing God's plan accepted His Will and the gospel of Jesus Christ now preached and granted to every human being. That is huge, God's plan touches more than our circle of influence; therefore, celebrating others and focusing on God helps us to understand the bigger picture.

How about this thought! Just maybe what you are asking for and you see manifesting in the lives of others is not what God has planned for you. Sometimes what we want and pray for is not the path that God has prepared for us. As believers and yet believers in God, we must understand and realize that His Will does not look like our will. Submission is the key. Know that God's Will is a higher plan that impacts more people, changes more lives, increases His Kingdom, and glorifies His name; thus, we must submit and surrender our will.

The Holy Bible illustrates a perfect example of how our plans may not be God's plan. In the account of King David, 2 Samuel depicts how David proposed to build a temple for God. In 2 Samuel, King David is talking with the prophet Nathan perplexed because, as a king, he lives in a palace while the Ark of God remains in a mobile tent (2 Samuel 7:1– 2), which in his mind is unsuitable for God. But the Word of the Lord came to Nathan, the prophet, and Nathan informs King David that God knows his "desires" to build Him a temple. But David will not be the person to perform this task because Solomon, his son (2 Samuel 7:12– 13; 1 Chronicles 28: 1– 6) will build the temple for God. In this story, God gave King David a specific command that what he desired to perform would not happen by his hands but by the hands of his son. King David had to celebrate future accomplishments that his son would execute for God. The blessing of building the temple belonged to his son, and King David had to accept God's plan not despising his son nor God. Contempt for either would be a question against King David's heart and motives. As in our journey, if we harbor any bitterness toward another person's blessing, we must question our motivation and character. If our desire is for self-gratification, then God was never in the plan. The book of James declares, we do not receive because we ask with wrong motives and personal pleasures, which have nothing to do with supporting others (James 4:3). But here is what King David charged his son with, which illustrates the heart of David and the call every person should seek. "And you, my son Solomon, acknowledge the God of your father, and serve him with wholehearted devotion and with a willing mind, for the Lord searches every heart and understands every desire and every thought. If you seek Him, He will be found by you; but if you forsake Him, He will reject you forever," (1 Chronicles 28: 9).

So, celebrate those around you whom God blesses, focus on and seek God's Will, and be ready for the time of your life because God blesses and honors His faithful children. Let His glory magnify.

6

Exercise Your Faith

Did you know that as you walk in the sun's direction, you will not see your shadow? But, when you walk with the sunlight behind you, this is when your shadow appears. Wow, I thought, this is a God revelation moment because I never paid attention to this before. On this beautiful sunny day, as I was walking on the trail in the heat of the day observing God's skilled hand in nature, He allowed an ordinary walk in the sun to become a teachable moment. I thought to myself, "Walking with God (*The Light*) diminishes self, my agenda, and my shadow. However, walking in the opposite direction of (*The Light*) God, I see my shadow representing self-image, self-gratification, and personal needs and wants existing." Yet, (*The Light*) is all around my small shadow. Therefore, God is always there and in control whether or not I focus on Him. Interesting observation, huh! Honestly, you may have already known this, but

God allowed me to take a typical everyday occurrence and view it with the eyes of the Holy Spirit.

Over the past few years, I have become very adamant about exercising. I love to take long walks and occasionally run on the trail. As I walk on the path, I become one with nature observing everything that God has created from the tall trees and swap areas to the insects, rabbits, squirrels, and deer. As I gaze at the woods, I see the hand of God, the Creator, thinking that humans could not have planted all those trees in the forest. Something higher than man and woman had to create this majestic scene. Walking on the trail provides seclusion, tranquility, and peace, an atmosphere that allows me to hear God's voice speaking to my heart and mind. And on this day, God gave me a greater understanding of walking in and out of the light.

So, "What does this have to do with exercising your faith?" It has everything to do with it because to observe nature and its various dynamics illustrates a supernatural paradigm that no human could construct. We must have faith to believe that God exists, and the God that created this world can most definitely handle our ordinary circumstances. My example of the sunlight and shadow show how walking in faith with God diminishes self to glorify Him. Anytime we seek to live our life without God, it guarantees an existence with struggles beyond our ability to bear. "I am the vine; you are the branches. If you remain in me and I in you, you will bear much fruit; apart from me you can do nothing" (John 15: 5) are the words spoken by Jesus Christ. Branches, vines, and fruit are a naturalistic analogy embedded in scripture but visible for the eye to see through God's creation. Just reflect on our human population where discord, destruction, depression, difficulty, disease, and a lot of other issues inhabit our surroundings. But the Bible tells us that wickedness surrounds our world, and the only way to overcome evil is by trusting God and having unshakable God-like faith. "I keep my eyes always on the Lord. With Him at my right hand, I will not be shaken" (Psalms 16:8). When we exercise our faith, we reveal that:

> ➢ *We trust God against all odds*
> ➢ *We cannot handle life without Him*
> ➢ *We need His protection, provision, and guidance*
> ➢ *We believe in what we do not see because He is leading us*
> ➢ *We know that no human can stop what God has pre-planned for our life*

Therefore, exercising your faith means you get to live stress-free because God is in control and taking care of all your needs. How do I know this? God's Word tells me this specifically in Matthew 6, verses 25–34:

> "Therefore I tell you, do not worry about your life, what you will eat or drink; or about your body, what you will wear. Is not life more than food, and the body more than clothes? Look at the birds of the air; they do not sow or reap or store away in barns, and yet your heavenly Father feeds them. Are you not much more valuable than they? Can any one of you by worrying add a single hour to your life? And why do you worry about clothes? See how the flowers of the field grow. They do not labor or spin. Yet I tell you that not even Solomon in all his splendor was dressed like one of these. If that is how God clothes the grass of the field, which is here today and tomorrow is thrown into the fire, will he not much more clothe you—you of little faith? So do not worry, saying, 'What shall we eat?' or 'What shall we drink?' or 'What shall we

wear?' For the pagans run after all these things, and your heavenly Father knows that you need them. But seek first his kingdom and his righteousness, and all these things will be given to you as well. Therefore do not worry about tomorrow, for tomorrow will worry about itself. Each day has enough trouble of its own."

God is telling you and I do not worry, trust me, and have faith in Him! If you seek God first, He will handle all the rest. I do not know about you, but I am relieved to know that God wants to take care of me. Now, I will be transparent to say that I have not always been this way, and some days it is hard to see God's Divine hand. But I believe this just comes with the territory of being human, housing an innate-spirit linked to God all-mighty.

I remember a time of stepping out on faith when I resigned from my job. I was having some serious personal and professional struggles with leadership; however, I remained because the job provided the salary, health benefits, and professional growth that I needed and wanted for myself and my family. I stayed at this job for three years, and each year was worse than the previous year. It seemed as if God would not work this situation out in my favor because He required more of me, which entailed exercising my faith and trusting Him instead of my paycheck, benefits, and 401k. God was taking me on a ride of self-independence to dependence on Him. During those three years, I lost weight, had anxiety attacks, sleepless nights, and eventually became depressed, but through those various emotional spells, I was physically healthy. I remember praying to God morning, noon, and night, all day to make it through each day of work. I would go to church three days a week and listen to church sermons daily to keep my sanity.

One day while I was sitting in my car, waiting for my son at soccer practice, I decided to listen to a church sermon hoping to build up my spirits. The message was titled, *"Come Back Kid."* I guess you can tell from the title of the message it was a sermon inspiring someone who needs to get back on that horse after being kicked down and stepped on. My work environment dampened my spirits so much I felt buried six feet underground even though my existence was above ground. After listening to this sermon, I played another message called *"Stay or Leave."* It was in that moment of listening to those two cd's that I knew what I had to do. God was speaking to me loud and clear, saying, "Get out of this rut! I have created you to be victorious! It is time to leave because you do not have the option to stay!" At that moment, God freed me of every burden and fear I was carrying between the harassment, loss of salary, benefits, and the uncertainty of my future. I could feel the weight of worry released from my spirit. Those work-related problems were no longer an issue, and my mind was free from anxiety. In that short hour of my son's soccer practice, I became a different person with a new attitude. It was as if the Holy Spirit said, "Enough is enough," so I went home, powered up my computer, and type up my letter of resignation. Oh, and I also had the best night's sleep ever in a long time. The next morning, I arrived early to work so I could give my boss my resignation letter, but he was not in his office, so I left the envelope on his desk and proceeded with my day. Even though I had two more months to work in this controversial environment, nothing fazed me; without a doubt, I knew that God was my shield and protector.

I did not know what my future looked like, nor did I worry because God had given me the peace to know that my decision was right. It was time for me to exercise my faith. I guess you would call it my Abraham moment. In Genesis, God told Abraham to leave his home and the place where his people dwell to a land that God would show him (Genesis 12:1). Abraham exercising his faith and belief in God left familiarity and comfort for what would become unfamiliar, and many times this is what God calls us to do. God wants us to step out of the boat, like Peter in Matthew 14: 22– 33, and walk on the water of Divine protection and provision toward impossible dreams and accomplishments achieved through His blanket of refuge. Know that fear consumed me because I was choosing not to live as societal normalcy from human logic to God's way of living. In no shape, form, or fashion does God's Word run perpendicular to what people say, and I know this to be true because if I said it, God would not receive the glory. God's glory magnifies against the odds. Are you familiar with the account of Gideon? It is one of many biblical truths where God defies the odds.

Scripture reads, "The angel of the Lord came and sat down under the oak in Ophrah that belonged to Joash the Abiezrite, where his son Gideon was threshing wheat in a winepress to keep it from the Midianites. When the angel of the Lord appeared to Gideon, he said, The Lord is with you, mighty warrior" (Judges 6:11– 12). Now, in just these two verses, we see first that Gideon is hiding from his oppressors because he is threshing wheat in a winepress. But to thresh wheat properly, an open field or space is necessary. Secondly the angel of the Lord addresses Gideon as a mighty warrior. However, in Gideon's mind, he is insignificant and weak, but the angel of the Lord tells him otherwise because that is how God saw him and sees us. As the story moves along, God wants Gideon to gather an army to defeat Israel's oppressors, the Midianites. Can you imagine Gideon's face or the thoughts running through his head? God, you want me to do what? Don't you see me threshing wheat in this winepress? I am not mighty, and I am from the weakest clan! Gideon was professing how he saw himself and what he was familiar with but not the unfathomed-ness of God's power.

Now you remember when I said God's glory magnifies against

the odds, and His Word is not perpendicular to human logic. In Judges 7, Gideon gathers his army of men as God instructed him. God tells Gideon in verse 2 that he has too many men, and some will need to return home. God's Word declares, "I cannot deliver Midian into their hands, or Israel would boast against me, my own strength has saved me" (Judges 7: 2). Gideon tells all the scared soldiers to go home, and twenty-two thousand men leave with ten thousand remaining. Again God informs Gideon that his army of soldiers is still too large; therefore, He must test their attentiveness with how they drink water. The men who drank water like dogs unaware of their surroundings got sent home, but those who cupped their hands and observed their environment remained. So Gideon was left with three hundred men when he started with roughly thirty-two thousand. "The Lord said to Gideon, with the three hundred men that lapped I will save you and give the Midianites into your hands" (Judges 7: 7). Human logic says, how can Gideon or any army win a war with three hundred men when they started with thirty-two thousand? <u>But, God! His Might! His Power! His Glory!</u> So, Gideon and his small army defeated the Midianites because God gave them the victory. Gideon had to exercise his faith in God and trust His Word. Gideon had to throw caution to the wind, human understanding, weak mentality, and insecurities to become the mighty warrior that the angel of the Lord called him (Judges 7).

Know and understand that we must respond in the same way as Gideon did thousands of years ago. Scripture informs us that "God is the same yesterday and today" (Hebrews 13:8), "God is not a man that He should lie" (Number 23:19), nor can "He be mocked" (Galatians 6:7). So if God required faith in His Word thousands of years ago, I believe wholeheartedly that He still requires us to have and show that same unwavering faith today. Is there something you need to let go, give up, stop doing, and trust God? Do It! Has God spoken His Word from the Heavens to your earthly realm and given you confirmation? Do It! Are you exhausted with your human efforts and need a supernatural miracle? Do It! Release the trust in what you <u>See</u> for what you do not <u>See</u>! As I write to you and you read this chapter, "exercise your faith" and know that God is with you!

PART III

The Future

7

Your Time Has Come

I do not know about your household, but living in a home with three men, my husband, and our two growing boys, I seem to visit the grocery store frequently. The ordinary stable items such as bread, milk, orange juice, lunch meat, eggs, cookies, and ice cream seem to disappear from the refrigerator and pantry weekly like magic. I know this typical list of items appears long, but with three men in the house, visiting the closest grocery store to stock up on essentials is a weekly chore. Once I complete my grocery list, I head to the self-checkout registers because I have noticed that those lines move quicker. I can get in and out of the store before I spend more money than I intended. I usually have a small cart or hand-cart, and once I find all my items, I head to the checkout line and wait for the next available opening. As I wait in line, I look intently for an open register to purchase my items. Aha! I see one; it is my turn! My time has come.

Christianity, "bought at a price" (1 Corinthians 6:20) by the blood of Jesus Christ is a freedom we all have access to, but we must first recognize our Lord and Savior and that our time has come. As I mentioned, when I stand in the self-checkout line, as you probably do the same, I look intently for an open register. My mind may wander toward the people passing by, the various sale items, or even the weekly magazine with the latest celebrity gossip; however, I am keeping my eye out for when my time comes.

When I say "your time has come," I'm not so much talking about you doing an extraordinary work for God as much as acknowledging His presence and Will for your life. I believe that recognizing God for who He is preceded your time coming. We can do nothing great or small in the economy of God without first yielding to His existence. How can we expect to do anything in the name of Jesus Christ if we do not know Him; thus, we must recognize before we administer? "Now this is eternal life that they know you, the only true God, and Jesus Christ, whom you have sent" (John 17:3).

When I say "your time has come," it may mean that you need to –

➢ *Transform your thoughts, ideas, and attitude*
➢ *Perform or take part in a service or ministry that gives God the glory*
➢ *Live a Christian life and be a witness for Jesus Christ through your life*
➢ *Help, love, serve, and give to others, thus, being that light we are all called to be*
➢ *Move-in the direction of your calling through the gift God has given you*

"Finally, brothers and sisters, whatever is true, noble, right, pure, lovely, admirable–if anything is excellent or praiseworthy- think about such things. Whatever you have <u>learned,</u> <u>received,</u> <u>seen,</u> or <u>heard</u> put it into practice. And the God of peace will be with you" (Philippians 4:8– 9).

When we read about the story of Abraham, he did not become the father of many nations until he recognized the one, true God. God spoke to Abraham and told him to leave the country where his family was living and move to a land unknown to him (Genesis 12:1). Scripture tells us that Abraham believed, and so he went, thus, recognizing his time had come. It was time for Abraham to leave the familiarity of his family's country and traditions for God to give him a new perspective. Therefore, this one simple act of obedience by Abraham sealed God's faithfulness not only to Abraham but to future generations, including you and I. God knew the heart of Abraham before Abraham surrendered to his calling.

Noah, a preacher of righteousness, was a man after God's heart. We learn that "Noah found favor in God's eyes and was considered a righteous, blameless man among the people in his time" (Genesis 6: 8– 9). God knew that He could trust Noah to build the ark before Noah even fathomed God's request. God, trusting Noah, and Noah obeying God meant that his time had come. It was time for Noah to move in the direction of his calling and God's purpose for humanity.

Moses, another servant of the Lord, had a call on his life that appeared to be prophetic from birth. In the days of Moses, baby boys were being killed according the king of Egypt's orders (Exodus 1:16). Since Moses was born during this proclamation, his parents hid him until they could no longer conceal his existence. They placed Moses in a basket and sent him down the Nile River, which Pharaoh's daughter found him (Exodus 2:1– 6). With Moses found by the king's daughter, one would think his death was inevitable.

He was an infant, Israelite boy fitting the description according to the king's orders, but the grace of God protected him. Little did Moses know that years of living as an Egyptian and learning their customs would be a future advantage for his true calling. God would call Moses some years later, after fleeing from Egypt, to free the Israelites from their oppressed conditions. Moses recognized God and responded to his call in the wildness. Moses yielded to God's presence, and his time had come.

In each of these accounts, Abraham, Noah, and Moses' time had come for them to be what God called them to be and do what God called them to do. They each had to acknowledge God as the one, true God believing that He existed and His Word was true. Each call was different, but the expectation of God's Word was the same. God expected each man to believe in what was unseen and unfathomable for his journey.

> ➢ *God asked Abraham to leave the comforts of his relative's home and land to travel somewhere unknown*
> ➢ *God asked Noah to build an ark when the people had never seen rain, especially floodwaters*
> ➢ *God asked Moses to free his people, the Israelites, when he lived for many years as an oppressor against them*

But before each man's calling, a time of recognition and obedience was necessary. The Bible tells us that Noah was a righteous man who had the favor of God (Genesis 6: 8– 9), but Abraham and Moses appeared to have God's trust before they knew Him. *So,* what does this say for you and me? I believe it means our time will come when we recognize God first then obey His command. As a generation made in the image of God but born from humans, we are all sinners (Romans 3: 9-10), and God knows that we're broken vessels. Broken with the ability to be used by God for His glory. We cannot work off a debt that the blood and sacrifice of Jesus Christ paid for us. When we know, we deserve nothing from God because of our sinful nature but seek to live as He has called us, this is when our time comes. We are open to allow God to transform our hearts, mind, and thoughts.

I knew my time had come when God's presence filled the emptiness and desperation in my heart. During that time in my life, I was going through so many emotions physically, mentally, financially, and relationally. It was as if I had run out of steam; I could no longer make hasty decisions because it occurred to me that my choices had dire consequences. When we walk the path that God has designed for us to take, I believe that it is a path that is simpler and less painful. The consequences are God proof; thus, we receive favor, grace, and mercy along the way. Some human-minded choices I have made had lasting effects, which I could have avoided. But what I can say for those lasting consequences is that they have become experiences that I can learn from and share with others. A scripture that comes to mind, which confirms that fleshly choices can produce future positive learning experiences, is Romans 8:28. "And we know that in all things God works for the good of those who love Him, who have been called according to His purpose" (Romans 8:28). So this tells me that my not-so-godly choices in the hands of God can still work out positive for me. Notice the scripture (v.28) says first "those who love Him," meaning we must know Him, secondly "called according to His purpose," meaning your time has come because He called you, and your obedience to Him will ultimately bring God glory.

However, understand that God gives us free-will. Various scriptures reveal humans as image-bearers of God, but we have the power to make our own choices.

> "This day I call the heavens and the earth as witnesses against you that I have set before you life and death,

blessings and curses. Now <u>choose</u> life, so that you and your children may live," (Deuteronomy 30:19).

➤ "But if serving the Lord seems undesirable to you, then <u>choose</u> for yourselves this day whom you will serve, whether the gods your ancestors served beyond the Euphrates, or the gods of the Amorites, in whose land you are living. But as for me and my household, we will serve the Lord," (Joshua 24:15).

➤ "If you <u>declare</u> with your mouth, 'Jesus is Lord,' and believe in your heart that God raised him from the dead, you will be saved," (Romans 10:9).

So, choose God, recognize His presence, and obey your calling because, through this obedience, your time will come.

8

Next Level Spiritual Maturity

Thump, thump, thump is the sound of my heart as I run on the nature trail near my home. The secluded, tranquil atmosphere of the path helps me to release the stress of the day, minimize the noise of traffic, and get away from the hustle and bustle of life. I can observe what God has created and become one with nature. I purposefully notice the various kinds of trees and animals and even the location and proximity of each tree. I begin to feel an overwhelming sensation that there has to be something higher than humans to design this creation of beauty. What person took the time to plant every tree and bush, carve out every swamp, place heaping stacks of gigantic rocks in a pile, or mount dirt into a 10-foot hill? No human, just God! The Bible tells us that God said, "Let there be light, water, sky, land, vegetation, living creatures, and humankind" (Genesis 1). Thus, the work of His hand is on the trail and everywhere. But on this ordinary day, as I was jogging, God gave me a different perspective toward observing His connection with His creation.

If you are a person who likes to exercise outdoors, have you ever noticed the varied styles of bikes? People ride single-seat one person bikes, bicycles that have two seats for two people to ride together, and then some bikes pull a carriage so a small child can ride along. Single bike riders can go at their own pace and speed. They are the navigator deciding whether to ride in a zig-zag formation, at the speed of light flying pass travelers, or a steady pace enjoying the atmosphere. However, two-seater bikes and bikes that pull a carriage are companion bicycles. People riding two-seater bikes have to pedal together, steer in the same direction, go at the same speed, and stop at the same time. If one person is pedaling and the other person is breaking, the bike will not work correctly. A two-seater bike has to move in motion with both people in sync. And a bicycle with the ride-along carriage has no choice but to enjoy the ride.

Despite all this, the point I am trying to make is that bikes with a double seat or carriage are like God and us. This life we live should be like a two-seater bike where God is in the driver seat directing us, steering us, and guiding us. If we allow God to be the captain of our life, as He should, He will steer us in the right direction, which leads us to next level spiritual maturity.

Next level spiritual maturity is what every Christian should seek to gain. This form of gradual daily development promotes godly peace in every area of your life–family, vocation, health, and spirituality. When I say the next level, I hope it is evident that growth and development have to take place. For example, when you get a promotion at work, you experience next-level thinking, networking, positioning, responsibility, and income. It comes with the territory! As Jabez prayed, "Oh, God, that you would bless me and enlarge my territory" (1 Chronicles 4:10). Thus, the economy of God is no different toward your thinking and responsibility levels. The Apostle Paul tells us, "Therefore, if anyone is in Christ, the new creation has come. The old has gone, the new is here" (2 Corinthians 5:17). As children of God, we cannot continue to walk on this earth sinning, disobeying, not spending quality time with God, using ungodly judgment and language, doubting, losing faith, or just not operating in the example and image of Jesus Christ. We have to *know* and *understand* that it is time to allow God to transform our thoughts and actions to produce next-level spiritual maturity. Apostle Paul declares, "Do not conform to the pattern of this world, but be transformed by the renewing of your mind" (Romans 12:2), which symbolizes next-level spiritual maturity. So what is spiritual maturity? Well, here are a few points to consider and include your thoughts.

Spiritual maturity is:

➢ *When you know that you have made a grave mistake and can own up to it, apologize, and move forward positively and productively. Be the bigger person and not harbor grudges, hatred, or bitterness!*

➢ *When you can, let your greatest failure become your most significant achievement!*

➢ *When you illustrate characteristics, such as integrity and commitment, and it becomes your way of living!*

➢ *When you put others before yourself; therefore, you receive joy in sharing their happiness!*

➢ *When you can withstand the tests and trials; thus, remaining on God's side, then your calling and time has come!*

➢ *When you can discern an answered prayer, whether "yes," "no," or "wait," and accept it because you know that God is in control!*

➢ *When you understand that spiritual maturity is continuous, never-ceasing, and always evolving, then you know that God is a God of constant revelation!*

Therefore, know that testing is the prerequisite to next level spiritual maturity. God tests those He loves, and through perseverance comes godly peace, discernment, and wisdom.

> "The Lord your God is testing you to find out whether you love Him with all your heart and with all your soul." (Deuteronomy 13: 3)

> "My son, do not despise the Lord's discipline, and do not resent His rebuke, because the Lord disciplines those He loves." (Proverbs 3:11)

> "But God disciplines us for our good, in order that we may share in His holiness... No discipline seems pleasant at the time, but painful; however, it produces a harvest of righteousness and peace for those who have been trained by it." (Hebrews 12: 10– 11)

Here's a great leader in the Bible called by God, given the gift of wisdom and leadership but tested, which later produced spiritual maturity. In the Book of Genesis, there was a young boy named Joseph. Scripture reveals that God spoke to Joseph through visions and dreams, which these prophetic encounters would change Joseph's life forever. God gave Joseph the gift of wisdom and leadership, but little did Joseph know that his predestined gift would come at the price of significant testing. In the accounts of Joseph, we learn that because of his dreams, his brothers detested him. They wanted to kill him, but they knew that their father loved

Joseph immensely. So, as the brothers' hatred built up because of Joseph's egocentric dreams, in their minds, they plotted to get rid of him. Scripture tells us they threw Joseph in a pit then sold him to the Ishmaelites, and the Ishmaelites sold him to Potiphar in Egypt (Genesis 37).

Now, my first thought toward the connection between God and Joseph was *"wow"* God is speaking to Joseph through dreams and visions, showing him how prosperous he will become. God is revealing to Joseph his future and what great things he will do. But, as Joseph's life unfolds, little did I think his brothers would sell him. On the contrary, Joseph was sold not once but twice, and as his life journey continued to spiral downhill, he ended up in prison. I did not see that coming as I read this account in the Bible, and I bet Joseph did not either. Can you say testing!

> ➤ *God tested Joseph with his dreams!*
> ➤ *God tested Joseph in the pit!*
> ➤ *God tested Joseph as his brother's sold him!*
> ➤ *God tested Joseph as he worked for Potiphar!*
> ➤ *God tested Joseph in prison!*
> ➤ *God tested Joseph's faith, loyalty, patience, humility, love, and the ability to forgive!*

Each trial that Joseph encountered, it tested his faith in knowing and believing in the dreams and visions God spoke into his life. Joseph had to stay focused on God and what He showed him, not giving into the circumstances of bondage, betrayal, denial, and envy. Each encounter developed Joseph's spiritual maturity so he would be patient in the process–*wait on God*, belief in the vision–*trust God*, die to self–*the character of God*, forgive and help others–*the heart of God*.

But through, notice I said *"through,"* Joseph's testing, he came out on the other side as refined gold (Zechariah 13:9) with the righteousness of God.

After spending a few years in prison, Pharaoh had Joseph summoned to interpret his dream. But before Pharaoh had this disturbing dream, Joseph interpreted the dreams of two men, which Pharaoh imprisoned, his cupbearer and bread maker. The dream interpretation for both men came true; therefore, they recognized Joseph as a man with godly wisdom. Sometime later, Pharaoh's cupbearer, out of his negligence, remembered that Joseph could interpret dreams, so Pharaoh had him summoned (Genesis 41: 9–13). God gave Joseph the wisdom and understanding to interpret Pharaoh's dream. Because of his accuracy, Pharaoh had Joseph released from prison and put in charge of Egypt's land and food supply for the future famine to come (Genesis 40 & 41).

So, what happened to Joseph's brothers since they initiated this spiral of mayhem events? Well, Pharaoh's dream was about a famine that would overtake the land, which Joseph had now become in charge of storing food for the people. As Joseph's family ran out of food, they had to come to Egypt for refuge. Thus, the prophecy of Joseph's dream came to fruition, but the tests and trials that Joseph sustained with the protection of God helped him to show the character, forgiveness, and love of God to his brothers and family.

In the Bible, there are various accounts of God-given gifts and talents given to many men and women, but each individual had to go through testing to refine their innate God-given character. So, if scripture illustrates this principle, which is exemplified through history, what makes us think we are any different or God has changed? "Jesus Christ is the same yesterday, today, and forever" (Hebrews 13:8); thus, God's expectation for our predestined gift, testing, and development is no different. "Remember your leaders, who spoke the word of God to you. Consider the outcome of their way of life and imitate their faith" (Hebrews 13:7). It appears to me that whether first-century Christian or modern-day Christian, the tone of this scripture delineates godly character, or shall I say next level spiritual maturity.

Now personally, next-level spiritual maturity has been a process, and I am still developing into that person God has called me to be. To the person I was 5, 10, or even 20 years ago, I spiritually matured. I can remember a time when it was hard for me to respect the opinions of my boss, especially if I thought what he or she said was unfair. I was always ready to retaliate and give that person a piece of my mind. The first time this happened, little did I know that I would work my entire shift only to end the day with a pink slip. And, my response was, *No Jesus, Just Flesh!* Had I known my boss would fire me that evening, I would have left after our confrontation, but he knew otherwise. The second time I gave my superior a piece of my mind, they asked me not to return to their establishment. Years ago, I used to work for the bank as a travel teller. On this particular day, my cash draw came up one cent short, and the head teller had to document it. I was annoyed because the error came from a roll of pennies I had acquired and opened from a customer.

I am kind of a perfectionist with things I take seriously, and work is one of them. So, instead of licking my wounds with a one-cent short drawer, I defended myself. Really, the word insubordinate is coming to mind. To make a long story short, they informed my immediate supervisor of my behavior, and I could no longer work at that branch. Again, *No Jesus, Just Flesh!* The third and last time I exhibited this behavior, my supervisor did not fire me, but he made my work environment a living nightmare.

It all started because I listened to the wrong advice and challenged my boss' decision. Did you catch that? I followed wrong counsel and challenged authority. That is a recipe for disaster whatever the situation. At my place of employment, there were a few open positions, which I was qualified to work, but my boss went with other candidates. Now he had the authority to go with whoever he chose, but the manner and credentials of his selected candidates did not follow policy guidelines; hence, the reason for me challenging his decision. You would think that I would have learned from my first encounter of using my words unwisely. No, I did not learn the first or second time but the third time was a charm. This is where God stepped into my life and said enough is enough. The tests and trials I received at that last job caused me to seek God daily crying out on bended knee. I may not have known Jesus Christ in those first two instances, but I was calling on the name of the Lord like a baby the last time around. Yes sir, *All Jesus!* And, this is when I can honestly say, my spiritual maturity began to develop. Even though my previous boss' may have been wrong or out of line in their actions or demeanor, they each still deserved my respect and subordinates. God showed me in His Word how I should interact with authority.

> "Submit yourselves for the Lord's sake to every human authority." (1 Peter 2:13)

> "Let everyone be subject to the governing authorities, for there is no authority except that which God has established. The authorities that exist have been established by God." (Romans 13:1)

> "Have confidence in your leaders and submit to their authority, because they keep watch over you as those who must give an account." (Hebrews 13:17)

"Remind the people to be subject to rulers and authorities, to be obedient, to be ready to do whatever is good, to slander no one, to be peaceable and considerate, and always to be gentle toward everyone." (Titus 3:1– 2)

Getting on my knees and crying for God's help, guidance, protection, and provision lead me to God's Word. I could not only recognize my offenses, actions, and ignorance but also understand that the battle was not mine but God's. Going blow for blow with authority made no sense. God granted each supervisor their power, and if he or she was acting out of character toward God's Will, it was not my responsibility to enlighten them in the manner I chose. Now, if mistreatment or discrimination is taking place, use proper protocol to handle that situation, but in my defense, it was time for me to close my mouth and keep my peace of mind to myself.

To this day, supervisors have overlooked my qualifications and skills for jobs, but because of my spiritual maturity, I have learned to let go and let God. My demeanor is humble, submissive, and respectful. I have learned that I cannot control anyone's actions and what God has for me is for me, and no human can stop it or take it away. Now, when something does not work out for me, I change my thought process to say, "God has something bigger for me to do!" So, if your next level spiritual maturity needs some tweaking because of your thought process, submit those ideas, behaviors, and attitudes to God so He can show you where He is trying to take you.

9

God Always Answers Prayers

In 1 Corinthians, the Apostle Paul says to the church of Corinth, "I gave you milk not solid food, for you were not yet ready for it" (1 Corinthians 3:2). If you continue to read this chapter, you will gather an understanding that Apostle Paul is focusing on worldly maturity versus spiritual maturity, which I discussed in the previous section. However, I want to take this verse beyond the physical context to a parallel imagery of how I see answered prayers.

When we pray to God, I would say that the majority of the time, our prayers are probably explicit. I know for myself; I pray for specific things. I may pray for healing for myself, coworkers, friends, family, a job or promotion, materialistic wants, children, spouse, protection/guidance from the enemy, and the list goes on. But whatever I pray for, it is catered to my needs. Now, when God answers your prayers, the big question is, do you recognize the answered prayer. I have heard in many church sermons and reading various Christian literature that God answers prayers in three different ways: yes, no, and later. A "yes" prayer comes in the form of what we asked for, and we thank God for answering our prayer with specificity. A "no" answered prayer is just that "no," and we cannot have it. I will say a "no" answered prayer sounds a little harsh, but what if it is in our best interest, saves us from hurt and pain, or redirects a dismal future, I appreciate God keeping me from what I cannot see. We need to thank God for what He foresees and knows before we encounter the hurt. A "later" prayer is one that we must wait on God as He develops our maturity. And this relationship is reciprocal because as we wait on God, He waits on us.

So, you say, "I get it, but what does all this have to do with milk and solid food?" As I share my understanding, you'll see that it has everything to do with it. When we can discern how God has answered our prayers, we mature from a milk understanding to a solid food understanding. I can bear witness to this now because when I first developed my relationship with God, my wisdom and discernment was milky. When I started reading the Bible, which was the King James Version (KJV), I did not understand it. The expression "a deer in headlights" comes to mind because the King James Version is slightly challenging to understand due to the audience and era it impacted. So praying and petitioning God was confusing and frustrating. I thought God did not hear or answer my prayers, but my understanding was immature. You know the pouting like a baby because I did not get that job, husband, house, etc. I would ask God, what does "later" mean? God, you're telling me I have to wait for something that I need right now! Come on! When I think about my novice spiritual maturity back then, I can say I was most definitely in the milky-way.

Now that many years have passed and my relationship with

God has grown, I have come accustomed to a meat and potatoes spiritual diet. But as flesh, which we are all human, I have reverted many times to the pouting syndrome because God did not answer my prayers. However, the understanding and wisdom God gave me has never left. Once you get and use, keyword *"use,"* God's wisdom, you do not lose it, but you can sometimes not want to accept it. Human temperament causes pride and ego to come to surface, but the Holy Spirit will always align us with the "fruits of the spirit" to encounter God's nature and will. Here are a few scriptures that illustrate God Answers Prayers.

> "This is the confidence we have in approaching God: that if we ask anything according to his will, he hears us. And if we know that he hears us— whatever we ask – we know that we have what we asked of him." (1 John 5:14– 15)

> "Again, truly I tell you that if two of you on earth agree about anything they ask for, it will be done for them by my Father in heaven. For where two or three gather in my name, there am I with them." (Matthew 18: 19– 20)

> "Jesus, replied, Truly I tell you, if you have faith and do not doubt, not only can you do what was done to the fig tree, but also you can say to this mountain, go, throw yourself into the sea, and it will be done. If you believe, you will receive whatever, you ask for in prayer." (Matthew 21:22)

> "If any of you lacks wisdom, you should ask God, who gives generously to all without finding fault, and it will be given to you." (James 1:5)

"Every good and perfect gift is from above, coming down from the Father of the heavenly lights, who does not change life shifting shadows." (James 1:17)

Now, by no means is this an exhausted list of prayer scriptures, but I am sure you see that God answers and wants to answer our prayers. But know that your prayers have to be according to His Will and character.

Hannah's Prayer

In the Book of Samuel, there was a lady named Hannah, wife to Elkanah, and he was the son of Jeroham. Elkanah had two wives Peninnah, who had children, and Hannah, who was childless (1 Samuel 1: 1–2). For years, Hannah did not birth any children while Peninnah birthed many sons and daughters to her husband. Having no children grieved Hannah's heart, and Peninnah did not make the situation any better because she continued to provoke Hannah (1 Samuel 1:3–7). Here's where a God answered prayer transforms Hannah's faith and life.

"In her deep anguish Hannah prayed to the Lord, weeping bitterly. And she made a vow, saying, Lord Almighty, if you will only look on your servant's misery and remember me, and not forget your servant but give her a son, then I will give him to the Lord for all the days of his life, and no razor will ever be used on his head." (1 Samuel 1:10–11)

Some things I recognized in Hannah's prayer:

➢ *She was weeping bitterly, a cry that pierced her heart and soul!*
➢ *She was desperate to have a child, particularly a son!*

> ➤ *She recognized God's Power and Authority!*
> ➤ *She made a vow to God, giving Him priority over her prayer!*
> ➤ *She knew that her vow to God would also require obedience!*
> ➤ *She called herself a servant of the Lord!*
> ➤ *She asked for God to remember and not forget her!*
> ➤ *She would submit her son to God and return the blessing He gave her!*

As I reflect on the dynamics of Hannah's prayer, she was seeking not only something personal to her needs and wants, but she also desired God's Will and nature within her prayer. Hannah saw herself as a servant of the Lord, so whatever the Lord blessed her with, she would have to serve the Lord with it. As the verses continue, the Lord remembered Hannah's prayer, and she became pregnant, gave birth to a son, and dedicated him to the Lord as she vowed (1 Samuel 1:19– 28).

From scripture, we can see that Hannah's prayer was specific, personal, and spiritual. Even though she desperately desired a child, she was willing to give what God gave her back to Him in praise. Just to incite thought right here! Whatever you pray for, are you ready to give it back to God? Are you willing to serve Him with it? Do you seek His direction for the growth and potential of it? If every gift is a blessing from God, then should not God get the glory and praise?

Hannah acknowledged God for the faithful Father He is. In her thanksgiving prayer to God (1 Samuel 2: 1– 11), she never mentioned her son. Samuel was the son she desperately prayed for, but in her prayer of praise and worship, she only thanked God for His faithfulness, power, sovereignty, strength, and love He showed her. Now that is some grown folk "solid food" praising. When you do not acknowledge the blessing by name, but the Creator for the gift.

Hezekiah's Prayer

Another story that might be familiar to you, which also reveals the power of an answered prayer by God is in the Book of 2 Kings. The Bible tells us that there was a king named Hezekiah, and he was gravely ill to the point of death (2 King 20: 1). The sickness that had taken over Hezekiah's body was fatal, and his death was imminent. But, before we go into Hezekiah's sickness and desperate prayer, I would like to focus on his family line and character for a moment.

Hezekiah was from the family line of Judah. He was the son of Ahaz king of Judah and after his father's reign, Hezekiah would become the next king (2 Kings 18:1). The family line of Judah were descendants of David who Samuel, the priest, anointed according to God's command (1 Samuel 16). When David was king, he sought God's wisdom all the days of his life. Like King David, Hezekiah loved and followed God. He prayed to God and pursued guidance and help from God with his decisions. "Hezekiah trusted in the Lord, the God of Israel. There was no one like him among all the kings of Judah, either before him or after him. He held fast to the Lord and did not stop following him; he kept the commands the Lord had given Moses. And the Lord was with him; he was successful in whatever he undertook" (2 Kings 18: 5– 7). I would say, like David, Hezekiah was a man after God's heart. Hezekiah trusted, clung to, followed, and obeyed God, thus seeking God's Will to ensure his success. Just to interject, "How's your relationship with God?" "Do you seek His wisdom and discernment for your life and decisions?" Scripture tells us that when the Assyria king spoke against the character and Will of God and the nation of Judah, Hezekiah prayed to God for His help. God answered Hezekiah's prayer and delivered him and his people from the Assyria king (2 Kings 19).

Sometime later, within Hezekiah's reign, he became ill. The

Prophet Isaiah told him he would die, and the Word of the Lord confirmed his death. Again Hezekiah prayed bitterly weeping to God to extend his life, "Remember, Lord, how I have walked before you faithfully and with wholehearted devotion and have done what is good in your eyes," (2 Kings 20:3); thus, as the Prophet Isaiah was leaving Hezekiah's home he returned to let Hezekiah know that the Lord had heard his prayer (2 Kings 20: 1– 6). Isaiah told King Hezekiah that God would spear his life 15 more years, and God would give a sign by making the shadow go back ten steps. So, not only did God answer Hezekiah's prayer and extend his life 15 more years, but God gave him a sign by showing him a shadow stepping backward (2 Kings 20: 6 – 11). Now, human logic tells us that our shadow moves forward in the direction in which we are walking. But God can defy the laws of nature and science; therefore, a shadow stepping back not just one step but ten steps undoubtedly is an act only possible with God.

So, "How's your prayer life?" One thing I have noticed from both accounts is that God answers desperate prayers. Hannah desperately wanted a son, and Hezekiah desperately wanted to receive healing. Scripture also reveals that both individuals trusted and believed in the living God to do what they asked and what no human could perform. They showed desperate faith for extraordinary results. Therefore, being of flesh and sinful nature did not exempt either person from God recognizing and answering their request because God knows there is no one perfect (Romans 3:10). He is always loving, gracious, and faithful.

As I reflect on the answered prayers illustrated in the Bible, I know full-heartedly that God is still in the business of answering prayers.

> *When I prayed for guidance within my decisions, God gave me direction!*

➢ *When I prayed for healing, God restored me!*
➢ *When I prayed for financial support, God gave me work, a supportive spouse, caring people to lend a hand, and a spiritual gift that would bless me immensely!*
➢ *When I prayed for a specific job, God gave me that job!*
➢ *When I prayed to homeschool, my son, God gave me the time, energy, and patience!*
➢ *When I prayed to support my children's education so they would not have debt, God supplied the financial means!*
➢ *When I prayed for support raising His children, God gave me His wisdom!*

I can go on and on about how God has answered my prayers, but I will say there have been some prayers that God did not answer and some prayers that I still await His confirmation. The unanswered prayers, which through discernment, I understand that God has said "no," which I have come to terms with trusting His decision. As I mentioned in chapter five when King David wanted to build a Temple for God, God told David that he would not be the king to build His Temple, but a king from his family line would undertake that prayer. God prohibited King David's request, and sometimes our prayers will also be denied. We have got to trust that God, who is the Alpha and Omega, beginning and the end, knows what is best for us. When we pray for things, we may not identify with the good or bad, maturity or ego, positive or negative, progress or stagnation our request will produce. Therefore, if God's answer is "no" or "wait," please understand He Knows what He is doing!

Let me leave you with a quote from L.B. Cowman's *Streams in the Desert* Devotional book. Reading this insight was very profound for me because I believe the key to our godly discernment is perspective.

"Every prayer of the Christian, whether for temporal or

spiritual blessings, will be fully answered if it meets certain biblical requirements. It must be prayed in faith and in accordance with God's Will. It must rely on God's promise, be offered up in the name of Jesus Christ, and be prayed under the influence of the Holy Spirit. Delayed answers to prayers are not only trials of faith; they also give us opportunities to honor God through our steadfast confidence in Him even when facing the apparent denial of our request."

10

Wait on the Lord

Waiting on the Lord is very important in our Christian walk, and every chapter I have written has illustrated some underlined gesture or perception that *waiting on God* is a requirement and unavoidable. Therefore, writing an entire section on this very subject was necessary because this simple action on our part is transformational in the economy of godly living. Godly living supposes to live by what is unseen and hoped for (Hebrews 11:1), which is not the custom of human logic because society says, "I will believe it when I see it." And with this thought process, we become anxious when "our" wants, goals, and plans do not seem to manifest according to the time-table we set. We ponder thoughts such as, "I'm 35 now and not married with children; I'm tired of working this dead-end job, when will my desired career goals come to fruition; I have the degree and skills, but why won't anyone hire me; I'm in this marriage that just does not work and I'm ready to leave; Everything I try to accomplish does not work out!" Do any of these scenarios sound familiar? If not, just place your thoughts with these suggestions, and you will get the picture.

Waiting on the Lord can be hard to do while living in a world that believes in instant self-gratification–providing us with a so-called standard of what the typical single or married life models. We try to live up to the expectations of society (our flesh) and not the Spirit, which is in tune with God's plan. Worldly expectations come at a price of worry, stress, depression, sickness, weariness, envy, competitiveness, idolatry, and a host of other issues that cause us to live beyond our means. However, when we live by the Spirit, we have a great promise and reward for *"waiting on the Lord."* Thus, living a life according to His Word, Will, Plan, and Power.

What I noticed about myself is that when I have a need that is not met according to my schedule, thoughts of God being absent, abandoning me, or me just not being worthy plague my mind. I began making moves and plotting solutions because I feel that I have reached a period of urgency. But God is not a God who watches or keeps up with time. "With the Lord a day is like a thousand years, and a thousand years are like a day" (2 Peter 3:8). Our perception of urgency does not alarm our Heavenly Father because He can change our situation with one spoken word. How do I know this to be true? The creation story gives us a broad illustration of how God can change an atmosphere with a simple spoken phrase.

Waiting on the Lord was a tendency humans lost when Adam and Eve ate the forbidden fruit. In the Garden of Eden, God gave Adam and Eve one boundary to obey, and that was to not eat from a specific tree. "And the Lord God commanded the man, You are free to eat from any tree in the garden; but you must not eat from the tree of the knowledge of good and evil, for when you eat from it you will certainly die" (Genesis 2: 16). Thus, disobeying God and eating from the tree of good and evil initiated humanity's downward spiral toward lack of faith, trust, dependency, and enthusiasm to waiting on the Lord. However, before the creation and disobedience of humans, God Himself illustrated the flawless characteristic of waiting on the Lord through the inception of Heaven and earth. The Book of Genesis 1 through 3 gives us a descriptive representation of how a formless, empty earth created and filled with matter came to existence (Genesis 1:1). We learn that God created everything on earth in six days and rested on the seventh day.

The beginning:

"In the beginning God created the heavens and the earth. Now the earth was formless and empty, darkness was over the surface of the deep, and the Spirit of God was hovering over the waters. And God said, "Let there be light," and there was light. God saw that the light was good, and he separated the light from the darkness. God called the light "day," and the darkness he called "night." And there was evening, and there was morning—the first day. And God said, "Let there be a vault between the waters to separate water from water." So God made the vault and separated the water under the vault from the water above it. And it was so. God called the vault "sky." And there was evening, and there was morning—the second day. And God said, "Let the water under the sky be gathered to one place, and let dry ground appear." And it was so. God called the dry ground "land," and the gathered waters he called "seas." And God saw that it was good. Then God said, "Let the land produce vegetation: seed-bearing plants and trees on the land that bear fruit with seed in it, according to their various kinds." And it was so. The land produced vegetation: plants bearing seed according to their kinds and trees bearing fruit with seed in it according to their kinds. And God saw that it was good. And there was evening, and there was morning—the third day. And God said, "Let there be lights in the vault of the sky to separate the day from the night, and let them serve as signs to mark sacred times, and days and years, and let them be lights in the vault of the sky to give light on the earth." And it was so. God made two great lights—the greater light to govern the day and the lesser light to govern the night. He also made the stars. God set them in the vault of the sky to give light on the earth, to govern the day and the night, and to separate light from darkness. And God saw that it was good. And there was evening, and there was morning—the fourth day. And God said, "Let the water teem with living creatures, and let birds fly above the earth across the vault of the sky." So God created the great creatures of the sea and every living thing with which the water teems and that moves about in it, according to their kinds, and every winged bird according to its kind. And God saw that it was good. God blessed them and said, "Be fruitful and increase in number and fill the water in the seas, and let the birds increase on the earth." And there was evening, and there was morning—the fifth day. And God said, "Let the land produce living creatures according to their kinds: the livestock, the creatures that move along the ground, and the wild animals, each according to its kind." And it was so. God made the wild animals according to their kinds, the livestock according to their kinds, and all the creatures that move along the ground according to their kinds. And God saw that it was good. Then God said, "Let us make mankind in our image, in our likeness, so that they may rule over the fish in the sea and the birds in the sky, over the livestock and all the wild animals, and over all the creatures that move along the ground." So God created mankind in his own image, in the image of God he created them; male and female, he created them. God saw all that he had made, and it was very good. And there was evening, and there was morning—the sixth day" (Genesis 1:1– 27, 31).

As you read these miraculous accounts of the creation story, you notice with each day God spoke it into existence. Before He gave anything the breath of life and existence, God commanded it first. Nothing happened until God gave the order for it to happen. So, what principle do you witness God, illustrating Himself as He created the reality of all things? *"He waits!"* We learn that:

> ➤ *God must command the situation; thus, nothing happened on the earth until He spoke it from Heaven!*
> ➤ *God is not in a rush because He took six days to create the earth when He could have spoken all things with one breath!*
> ➤ *God took pleasure in what He created admiring its beauty as He said each day's creation was "good!"*
> ➤ *God believes in resting since there was evening and morning between each creation and an additional day of rest.*
> ➤ *God is a God of order, reflection, and multiplication!*

Now scripture reveals that God is the same yesterday, today, and forever (Hebrews 13:8), and there are thousands of years between the Old Testament creation account and the New Testament. When God sent His one and only Son, Jesus Christ, to die for our sins (John 3:16), He too showed the value of *waiting on the Lord.*

Theologians consider the Book of John a Gospel account because it illustrates the life of Jesus Christ. Even though Jesus Christ died for our sins, He also portrayed the characteristics of a Christian believer, leaving an example for us to imitate. In the Gospel of John, I noticed a few incidents of how Jesus Christ is showing the principle of *waiting on the Lord* for us to observe and learn. In chapter 2 of the Book of John, Jesus Christ, His mother, and the disciples are attending a wedding. During the celebration, the people run out of wine and Jesus' mother makes an interesting appeal to her son. "When the wine was gone, Jesus' mother said to him, "They have no more wine." "Woman, why do you involve me?" Jesus replied. "My hour has not yet come." His mother said to the servants, "Do whatever he tells you." Nearby stood six stone water jars, the kind used by the Jews for ceremonial washing, each holding from twenty to thirty gallons. Jesus said to the servants, "Fill the jars with water"; so they filled them to the brim. Then he told them, "Now draw some out and take it to the master of the banquet." They did so, and the master of the banquet tasted the water that had been turned into wine. He did not realize where it had come from, though the servants who had drawn the water knew... What Jesus did here in Cana of Galilee was the first of the signs through which He revealed His glory; and His disciples believed in Him" (John 2:3-9, 11). When Mary mentions the wine is gone, Jesus stated, "Woman, why do you involve me, my hour has not come yet" (John 3:4). Jesus knew her intentions before making her request known. Thus, He demonstrated patience and obedience before performing any miracles. Jesus showed us the importance of "waiting." His reaction in calling His mother *woman* revealed her human urgency and impulsive motives, which many of us display when we feel the need or desire for something. But reluctantly, Jesus did what His mother requested and performed His first miracle according to scripture, and God received the glory.

What about when Jesus' brothers told Him it was time to stop hiding in secret so He could become a public figure in chapter 7 of the Book of John? "Jesus' brothers said to him, "Leave Galilee and go to Judea, so that your disciples there may see the works you do. No one who wants to become a public figure acts in secret. Since you are doing these things, show yourself to the world." For even his own brothers did not believe in him. Therefore Jesus told them, "My time is not yet here; for you any time will do. The world cannot hate you, but it hates me because I testify that its works are evil. You go to the festival. I am not going up to this festival, because my time has not yet fully come." After he had said this, he stayed in Galilee. However, after his brothers had left for the festival, he went also, not publicly, but in secret" (John 7:3– 10). Jesus did not need the approval of the world because He came to save the world. He only needed to wait on the Lord's timing so that God would get the glory, and more people would receive salvation and believe. If you continue to read this chapter in the Bible, you will see that Jesus showed up to the festival on His terms and proclaimed the Word of God (John 3: 14), so God's timing trumped His brother's opinion.

Or, how about the account of Jesus raising Lazarus from the dead, a unique healing, which Jesus had never performed? Many of the people witnessed Jesus heal the sick, blind, and lame, but Lazarus would be the first account of someone rising from the dead. Scripture tells us that Mary, Martha, and Lazarus were close friends of Jesus, and He even dined at their home (John 11: 5). However, one day Lazarus became ill, and his sisters sent word by messenger for Jesus to come and heal him. Once the messenger arrived to the town Jesus was visiting and informed Him of the state of Lazarus' illness, Jesus did not leave immediately. Instead, Jesus remained in the same place for two more days after hearing about Lazarus. "When He heard this, Jesus said, 'This sickness will not end in death. No, it is for God's glory so that God's Son may be glorified through it… So when He heard that Lazarus was sick, He stayed where He was two more days" (John 11: 4– 7). From the mouth of Jesus, He tells the disciples that this condition is for God's glory, a blatant indication that He was waiting on the Lord and we are to do the same thing. Jesus, as God in the creation story, was in no rush or anxious about anything.

> ➢ *Jesus knew that Mary and Martha expected Him to heal Lazarus from his illness as He had done for others!*
> ➢ *Jesus knew it bewildered the disciples at His choice to delay leaving instead of rushing to heal a close friend!*
> ➢ *Jesus knew that human logic would deem death as the ending with no immediate resurrection!*

➤ *Jesus knew that raising Lazarus from the dead would strengthen the believer and yet believer!*

➤ *Jesus knew that the miracle of Lazarus would reach the religious leaders and His haters!*

➤ *Jesus knew fully that His purpose on earth was to bring God glory!*

So, yes, Jesus waited on God because every miracle He performed God was to receive the glory. Jesus and God are one in unity, and with the examples Jesus illustrated, God wants us to be one with Him. So, maybe just maybe your obedience to waiting on the Lord will magnify and reveal God's glory in your situation. When we operate in the purpose, plan, and Will of God, He always gets the glory. But, this glory should not only strengthen your belief in Him; God wants His miracles and blessings to touch the hearts and minds of others around you so that more people come to know Jesus Christ.

Waiting on the Lord means we must trust and believe in Him fully. We must make a conscious resolution in our hearts to trust that no matter the circumstance, whatever the situation, He will be there and help us. "But seek first His kingdom and His righteousness, and all these things will be given to you as well" (Matthew 6: 33). Jesus tells us not to worry but seek and believe in Him, and not some, but all our needs will be met.

I aim always to trust God, but several times in my life, when a storm appears, I have reverted to doubting and worrying. With many sleepless nights tossing and turning, I think about why things are not working out, and how I can fix it. I ask God questions like:

➤ *If you brought me to this situation then why are you not helping me?*

➤ *If you are with me why can't I feel your presence or see your provision?*

> ➤ *Why can't I see your hand working this situation out?*
> ➤ *Lord, why have you given me so many burdens to bear?*

But in all honesty, the only way I regain focus and calm my thoughts is by standing on His Word and seeking His presence. I stop and ask God, what are you trying to teach or show me? Help me become a quick learner! Give me your wisdom, discernment, and understanding so I may *know* and *move* in your Will for my life. As I change my thought process toward God and not my situation, I begin to feel peace and assurance over my soul. I focus on the impossible with a mindset that it is only possible with God. I tell myself that what the world deems is correct or customary is not what God says because "our thoughts are not God's thoughts and our ways are not His ways" (Isaiah 55:8). My obedience and faith will look peculiar and out-of-place to humans, and myself, but that is when I assuredly know that I am not operating in my strength or knowhow. I remind myself that God's Word says, "He will never leave me or forsake me" (Hebrews 13:5). Where God leads, He feeds; Where God guides, He provides! To receive a supernatural, miracle from God, your circumstance has to be beyond your control, and you must stay the course to receive the blessing and testimony!

As I write these thoughts to uplift your spirit, I am also building mine. I am waiting on the Lord just like you for a supernatural miracle right now. Presently, I work at a private Christian school as a teacher, which my younger son also attends this school. When I enrolled him into the school, I was working with two educational institutions, which both incomes provided the means for our household and for him to attend this private school. While working in this Christian environment, I embraced the atmosphere, which invoked prayer, devotion, worship, respect, love, and the oneness of God for each other. Being a part of an educational setting that endorsed these activities, I saw my other job as a distraction from my real purpose. So, I prayed and asked God to remove the "good" distraction, which was the other school I was working for, so I would be more available to walk in the destiny He had for me. Well, that is just what God did? After a year of working at the Christian school along with my other teaching position, and my son attending the private school, I lost that teaching position that I prayed to God about removing.

Now to back up a little. Before accepting the position at the Christian school, my primary employer merged with another educational institution; thus, it was a matter of time before cuts back and position eliminations would take place to save company revenue. However, I thought my teaching position was secure because teachers are the foundation of any educational institution and without teachers there are no students. Likewise, without students, there is no need for teachers. But!!! Yes! You guessed it, management eliminated my position, and I lost my job, benefits, and salary. I was not disappointed because I had prayed for this job transition; however, I was nowhere ready for the whirl-wind of financial problems that would come with it, one being my younger son's private educational stability. So, what would a person say to do in this situation? Just take your son out of private school and place him back in public school! He's been in public school before, and he will be fine! Save that money because private school tuition is expensive!

But what does God say about this situation? Did I not lead you to this Christian school? Was this an answered prayer? Why would I bring you to and not through this storm? Did you pray to place your son in a better, Christian learning environment? Do you not trust in Me to make a way? Why are you looking at money? Doesn't My Word say, "You cannot serve both God and money" (Matthew 6:24). Just obey and have faith in Me! I am your security and source!

Seek your purpose and My plan because that is where your resource lies! Your gift will make room for you! These are the questions God places in my heart and mind every time I make a conscious decision to follow my human logic instead of God's unfathomed thoughts. Please know and remember that God's choices will look unheard of to a person!

So, my son has completed three years in a private Christian school environment, and I am trusting God for his continued attendance. I am *"waiting on the Lord"* and not looking at the bleakness of my circumstance. I am trembling and trusting God only because I know He placed my son and me at this school. Both of us being in this environment was an answered prayer, but as I mentioned before, God tests His children. And I believe that I am in a period of testing to see if I will stand on His Word or listen to human reason and look at my situation as hopeless. Will I let anxiousness and worry be the motivation for rushed decisions with lasting consequences? Will I miss the supernatural miracle and blessing that God wants to give my family and me, which will change our lives forever! Know that an answered prayer and God command goes hand-and-hand with a test of faith. Anytime God gives us a command, and we obey, He will test our faith because our security is now in Him and not in what we can see. In actuality, our security has always been in Him, but we must acknowledge His presence and allow the Holy Spirit to lead.

Hebrew 11 illustrates various men and women who took a leap of faith in God but tested and received the victory for their perseverance. So, what is "faith?" "Now faith is confidence in what we hope for and assurance about what we do not see and the ancients were commended for it" (Hebrews 11:1–2).

> "By faith Noah, when warned about things not yet seen built an ark at the command of God."

> ➤ "By faith Abraham, obeyed and went to a place unknown to him at the command of God."
> ➤ "By faith Sarah, conceived a child past her childbearing age."
> ➤ "By faith Abraham, when God tested him, offered Isaac as a sacrifice."
> ➤ "By faith Moses left Egypt not fearing the king's anger because he saw Him who was invisible."
> ➤ "By faith the Israelites passed through the Red Sea on dry land."
> ➤ "By faith the walls of Jericho fell." (Hebrews 11:1– 30)

And there is much more to share about the faith-acts many other god-fearing men and women performed because they trusted the God of what is impossible with humans being possible with Him!

Just think, Jesus commanded the disciples to follow Him. They withstood many tests as they walked with Jesus, but little did they know there would be greater tests and challenges to overcome once Jesus died for our sins, rose from the dead, and ascended to the right hand of the Father. The test of their faith would become more significant in a world where the gospel was *"new!"* If the disciples did not withstand the test of time, you and I would not have access to the good news of the gospel now! Jesus knew that they would persevere, and you must endure too!

Even though the Bible gives us many renditions of men and women waiting on the Lord, some made grave mistakes in the process of keeping the faith. But what better way for Christians to understand the principle of waiting on God than watching God in action, and I think the creation of the earth is enough to know that God is in control. All things will happen in your life at just the right time as you wait on Him! So, whatever you are worried, stressed, frustrated, weary, feared, disappointed, or any other negative emotion, do not succumb to that way of thinking. God is with you and will deliver you! Discernment is the key to waiting and making the right choices. God's wisdom will tell you when to Stop, Go, or Wait!

So be encouraged in our living, omnipotent, ever-present Heavenly Father. He is just a prayer and a "pause" away from healing you, helping you, delivering you, and saving you in the precious name of Jesus Christ, Our Lord, and Savior!

Are You There God? The answer to that question is "yes." Scripture tells us that God has predestined our future, and with a predestined fate comes the maze of life that God has planned for us to walk (Romans 8:30, Ephesians 2: 10). If we pay close attention, we can see how God is constructing circumstances to build our character, weaknesses, wisdom, discernment, and dependency on Him. As each chapter reveals some of my trials, my understanding and maturity transformed with every phase of life. The person I am today believes in trusting and stepping out on faith in God.

Reflection Questions

Introspection is the key to understanding where you are now, where you are going, and if redirection is necessary. When you reflect on past decisions, actions, and outcomes, you can see how God's hand has guided and directed you. Even if your choices have worldly motives, a new, godly mindset can help you witness God's provision and protection in your mess. As I have taken this time to share my trials, test, and maturity, I hope it leads you to not only reflect on your life but also to commit to making those necessary changes, so you mirror the example of Jesus Christ.

> "Therefore, if anyone is in Christ, the new creation has come: The old has gone, the new is here! All this is from God, who reconciled us to himself through Christ and gave us the ministry of reconciliation: that God was reconciling the world to himself in Christ, not counting people's sins against them. And he has committed to us the message of reconciliation. We

are therefore Christ's ambassadors, as though God were making his appeal through us. We implore you on Christ's behalf: Be reconciled to God. God made him who had no sin to be sin for us, so that in him we might become the righteousness of God." (2 Corinthians 5:17– 21)

Chapter One: I Did Not Really Know Him Back Then

- ❖ Do not be embarrassed if you do not know or yet believe in Jesus Christ. Reading this book means that you are seeking something other than what you see or what society has to offer. So, how does God, whom you did not recognize, make Himself known to you?
- ❖ When I first learned about Jesus, I was young, maybe 4 or 5 years old. At this age, I was not mature enough to understand our living God. My spirituality was ritual-based from a parental expectation of attending church. So, do you know God because of what you experienced growing up in your parent's home? Has this caused a spiritual gap between your younger years and adult years? What caused the lack of connection toward your growing relationship with God?
- ❖ I mentioned in my book that as I grew older, I only knew God as an occasional night time prayer and blessing over food. Other than that, I did not address God as my source, helper, guide, protector, or provider. How do you know God is in your life? Do you want to see more of Him in your life, and how can you make that happen?

Chapter Two: Every Tub Has to Sit on Its Own Bottom

❖ I believe this topic is relevant for every human being living on this planet. We all have to be accountable for our actions with needs, wants, goals, dreams, and results. Our parents seek to help us in our life journey to become young adults. Then history repeats itself as we become parents. But self-control is the key to knowing when enough is enough, and when as parents, we have to let our children live their life. So, how's your self-control, or do you have to be in control of everything?

❖ God is in control of everything, and nothing happens in your life or your children until God is ready. God gives us wisdom to share, but we should not abuse this wisdom focusing on other's abilities and goals, thus stagnating our purpose. So, are you the person who can always be so diligent in helping others with their goals but sometimes lack the tenacity for yourself? Have you ever wanted something so bad for someone else, but they chose a different direction? How can their choices help you reflect on your future and move on to your goals?

❖ Broken focus is a distraction toward your God-given gift. The more attention you place on others, the less attention you give to God to transform your life. Where are you experiencing broken focus? How can you redirect this energy toward what God has for you?

Chapter Three: Reflect on the Past but Do Not Stay There

❖ Our past is something that can hinder our growth potential and future. When we allow feelings and thoughts to keep us in the past, we cannot see what God has placed right in front of us to possess. Know that reflection on the past is necessary to change your direction and future. But if you stay too long, it becomes a distraction and hindrance to your growth. So, what happened in your past that has you stuck? How can you let go and move forward? Reflect for a moment, find the root cause, repent or forgive, and plan a different course of action for progression.

❖ The Bible tells us to confess our sins to one another and pray for each other, so that we will be healed (James 5:16). Understanding this, we cannot honestly get passed our past unless we confess it, forgive, and pray. Even though reflection on the past creates awareness and ownership, what I feel is significant is healing. Healing opens us up to love, try, believe, and trust again. So, do you need to seek counsel to help with healing? Do you need to forgive someone or receive forgiveness? Is it time to get on your knees and ask God to come into your life for your ultimate healing?

Chapter Four: What Did God Tell You to Do Last

❖ When you have to reflect on what God told you to do last, you will either feel resentful or remorseful if you did not obey. Each emotion is a feeling that God did not design or want us to entertain. However, when we choose not to listen and exercise our free-will, the consequences we endure can either pose a negative feeling on us or toward God. The questions I have posted here come from the chapter text. Take the time to write each answer, reflect, and ask God for guidance and clarity.

Are you running from your God-given gift?

Are you replacing a command with comfort?

Has your lack of follow-through toward what God told you to do last, affected your family, significant others, or those around you?

Is disobeying God worth the affliction imposed on yourself or others?

Has your disobedience caused others to experience loss, whether physically, mentally, emotionally, spiritually, or financially?

Has your noncompliance to God's Will caused others to feel sorry for you and try to help you? Did their empathy change your outcome?

Have the efforts of others been unsuccessful; thus, manpower is no power against God's power?

What are you going to do NOW?

Chapter Five: Do Not Focus on the Blessings of Others, Celebrate

❖ The grass is not greener on the other side. If it appears that way, it is either a façade or being nurtured. Your best call to action would be to cultivate your grass with the guidance of the Holy Spirit, so you bear fruit (John 15). So, how can you make better decisions, actions, and reactions? How can you redirect your focus from coveting the lives of others? What can you do to put more effort into your spirituality, home, marriage, job, children, ministry, etc.?

❖ I have heard before that when things are not going right in your life, help someone else. The joy they experience will uplift your spirit. Who can you help today or this week?

Who can you pray for today or this week? Who can you be a blessing to even in your struggles?

❖ As you reflect on your life experiences and how they may have encouraged someone else's success, never devalue being a conduit for God because you never know what God is doing behind the scene. What blessings did you receive that you did not notice because of your misplaced focus? How did God bless you in your blind-spot thinking?

Chapter Six: Exercise Your Faith

❖ "Faith is the confidence in what we hope for and the assurance of things unseen" (Hebrews 11: 1). How does this verse speak to your heart? Has God given you the sensation that He is a God who operates in an unknown realm to the human mind? My heartfelt feelings are that I cannot adequately put my trust in what I see. Whatever is recognizable to the eye is temporal and ever-changing. Tangible things provide no assurance, but God and His nature, provision, protection, guidance, and salvation are full-proof. So, how's your confidence toward what you hope to obtain? When you do not see your need met, do you still have assurance? Do you believe in the Word and Power of God?

❖ I will say that your "faith" determines your progress and position spiritually and earthly. Faith is the kinetic energy to your perseverance, encouraging a steadfast spirit that waits to see God's supernatural unfold. Scripture tells us, "Without faith it is impossible to please God" (Hebrews 11:6). God, a Spirit-Being connects with our spirit in an unseen manner to the human eye but felt in our inner-being unexplainable and undeniable. So, how do you plan to release your faith in God? Is there something you need to let go, give up, or stop doing to trust God? Has God spoken His Word from the Heavens to your earthly realm and given you confirmation? Are you exhausted with your human efforts and need a supernatural miracle? Believe, Trust, and Have Faith!

❖ It is essential to understand that faith and trust go hand in hand. When you say that you trust someone (friend, spouse, relative, coworker, any close relationship), what is it about the person that makes you trust them? Is it based on them keeping their word or promise; you can witness their actions or diligence; does experiences or history with that person play a role? Our trust and faith in God should be no different, but actually, it is different because we are walking with confidence and trust in the unseen. We are moving, breathing, and living through an anticipatory relationship where miracles and supernatural power can only materialize through faith, obedience, testing, then blessing. If your trust is in an individual before God, how will you change that? Do you see a need, and if not, why? What is it about trusting God, who is unseen that scares you?

Chapter Seven: Your Time Has Come

❖ As I ponder the questions to ask for this chapter, some relevant life experiences and thoughts come to mind. To know your time has come, you have to recognize God's existence and presence. But what is also instrumental to your newfound awareness is moving when that time comes. Be committed, determined, and disciplined to see whatever it is to the end. If God reveals Himself to you and gives you revelation, do not waste time acting on His command or your answered prayer. Has God given you a command, but you have not moved on it? If days, weeks, months, or years have gone by, what do you plan to do now? You know, as long as you have breath in your body, you still have time?

❖ When God reveals Himself in your situation, burden, or circumstance, this is the time to change your attitude, actions, decisions, focus, and life. If we do not take the time to observe and act on how God's Divine hand is manipulating our situation, our life will stay the same. What factors in your life cause you to neglect or forget God's revelation in your life? If you tried things your way, how's that working out for you? Do you feel that your life is stagnant? What do you plan to do now?

❖ When your time comes, know that this is God speaking to you. Know that He wants to reveal hidden secrets to you (Isaiah 45:3), change your life, the direction of your path, and become a relevant part of your future. If you are reading this book, "Your time has come!" Now Act!

Chapter Eight: Next Level Spiritual Maturity

❖ With each year we grow older, there is a rational expectation that we develop in maturity. Our thoughts and actions at five years old should be different when we're ten years old. And how we thought and acted at ten years old should be changed when we're fifteen years old. I think you get the picture. So, if human logic expects developmental maturity from year to year, what do you think God expects. We go from baby food to solid food, crawling to walking and running, riding a bike to driving a car, single to married, childless to parenthood, and the list goes on and on. However, as we grow in our spiritual maturity, our attitude should illustrate a never-ceasing progression. Being patient in the process–*waiting on God*, believing in the vision–*trusting God*, dying to self– *the character of God*, forgiving and helping others– *the heart of God*. Maturity starts with mentality, how's your mental state? Are your roots grounded in people, materialistic things, money, or God? Are you building a house on the "rock" or sand (Matthew 7:24–27)?

❖ Next level spiritual maturity requires an intimate relationship with God. Life is hard, and things happen, but God does not want your faith in Him to waver. He wants you to depend on Him and only Him as your source, provider, protector, shield, fortress, healer, and deliverer. As you seek to spend time with God, let me give you some scriptures to meditate on (Psalm 91, Matthew 6:25 – 34, John 15). How are these scriptures building your trust and faith in God?

Chapter Nine: God Always Answers

❖ Prayer is a Christian connection to God, but God's ears are sensitive to every human being because He created us in His image (Genesis 1:28). He longs for His Word to be preached, practiced, and proclaimed to the ends of the earth (Mark 16:15). So, how's your prayer life and relationship with God? Do you seek His wisdom and discernment for your life, physical and spiritual maturity, and decision-making? Will you give God the glory and praise for His faithfulness to you?

❖ I have learned over the years that we must be very vigilant and cognitive to what the Holy Spirit is saying and where He is leading us. God always hears our prayers and answers them. Sometimes an answered prayer will come in the form of something we did not expect. If you need proof, read 2 Kings 5 about Naaman the Leper. He had expectations about how his healing would take place, and God's prophet met none of those expectations. But he received a supernatural miracle. If we are not attentive to His voice and subtle nudges, we will miss how God is replying to our need or want. Are you sensitive to the Holy Spirit? How would you know if God answered your prayer?

❖ What I have learned and noticed in the Bible is that God not only answers prayers, but He also answers desperate prayers. In your desperation, who do you seek first, a person, or God? Whatever you pray for, are you willing to give it back to God? Are you ready to serve Him with it?

Chapter Ten: Wait on the Lord

❖ I know you're anxious. Anxiousness is a feeling that every person illustrates because we make plans, set goals, and have expectations for what "we" want to come to fruition. But how do you handle rejection? Are you flexible and adaptable? If not, you will soon find out that your plans will sometimes have to take a backseat to what God has planned. Scripture states, "Many are the plans in a person's heart, but it is the Lord's purpose that prevails." (Proverbs 19:21) So, what are you waiting on God to answer? How can you become a steadfast spirit faithful to God's timing?

❖ Have you ever heard the cliché, "When life throws you lemons, make lemonade?" How can you be resilient in the waiting, trial, storm, or test? What if you do not get what you want, will this change your attitude toward life or God? Turning from God will show what you truly value.

❖ In the Bible, many men and women waited years to receive specific blessings from God. Abraham received the promise of Isaac at seventy-five years old, but the birth of this son did not happen until Abraham was one hundred years old. That is twenty-five years! Joseph had dreams of his brothers bowing down to him when he was a young boy. The image of his dreams did not manifest for several years. Joseph was a grown man when the famine took place, and his brother's bowed at his feet. Are you willing to wait 3, 5, 10, 20 years for God's Divine plan for your life? If not, why? If so, what can you do in the meantime? Who's plan is more meaningful yours or His?

About the Author

Charisse Jones is a Christian, wife, mother and educator. She has eighteen years of teaching experience and has been blessed to work with all ages from preschool to college level. Charisse is also a blog writer and created her own website, devotionspirit.com. She is passionate about ministering God's Word through teaching and writing to help others encounter the presence, wisdom, and love of God.